Annie Ernaux

La Place

Tony Jones

Lecturer in French
University of Southampton

Une femme

Loraine Day

Lecturer in French
University of Southampton

UNIVERSITY OF GLASGOW
FRENCH AND GERMAN PUBLICATIONS
1995

University of Glasgow French and German Publications

Series Editors: Mark G. Ward (German)
Geoff Woollen (French)

Consultant Editors: Colin Smethurst
Kenneth Varty

Modern Languages Building, University of Glasgow,
Glasgow G12 8QL, Scotland.

This book is dedicated to Mary and Jim,
and to the memory of Erica, Lewis and Jess.

First published 1990; reprinted 1995.

Printed by BPC Wheatons, Ltd., Exeter.

ISBN 0 85261 262 1

Contents

Preface

Bracketed page numbers in **bold type** refer to the Gallimard 'Folio' editions of *La Place* (no. 1722) and *Une femme* (no. 2121), whose pagination is identical to that of the original Gallimard editions. When cross-references are made, and in the Glossary, they are respectively indicated in the following manner: **(P,**114); **(F,**81).

We should like to take this opportunity to express our gratitude to Annie Ernaux for her friendly and very constructive interest in our work. We also wish to thank Janice Carel and Cécile Velu, who cheerfully helped us to track down the more obscure textual references. Finally, Graham, Hannah, Sam and Jessica deserve special thanks for their support and understanding.

Loraine Day   Tony Jones

Introduction

Annie Ernaux was born in 1940 in Normandy to the owners of a
café-épicerie. She obtained a first degree at Rouen University,
and subsequently qualified as a secondary school teacher. She
has taught in Annecy and near Paris, and now combines her
work as a writer with teaching for the C.N.E.C. (Centre
National d'Enseignement par Correspondance). She was
awarded the Prix Renaudot for *La Place* in 1984.

In addition to *La Place* (1983) and *Une femme* (1987),
Ernaux has published three novels—*Les Armoires vides* (1974);
Ce qu'ils disent ou rien (1977); *La Femme gelée* (1981)—and
two recent works of fiction of a more hybrid variety—*Passion
simple* (1991), and *Journal du dehors* (1993). All her works draw
in different ways on her personal experience and all are first-
person narratives, although *La Place* and *Une femme* differ
from the three earlier works by the way in which they
specifically foreground the work of literary composition,
recording the narrator's hesitations and choices as a writer,
and point towards the connexion between the creative
endeavour and the quest for fresh insights and understanding.
It must, however, be stressed that Ernaux's works are not
straightforwardly autobiographical. In her novels, fictional
elements are used freely, and the more overtly 'authentic'
narratives of *La Place* and *Une femme* focus as much on the
narrator's father and mother, and indeed on family history and
circumstances, as on the narrator herself. Hence they may be
said to have, in addition to the autobiographical, a
biographical or documentary dimension.

The exploration of relationships and social context is only to
be expected from a writer who stresses, as Ernaux does, that
the individual is firmly rooted in a particular milieu and
historical moment. Nor should the presence of fictional
elements be thought to be incompatible with the
autobiographical project, if by autobiographical we refer to the
author's bid, through the process of writing, to understand and
express her own experience and the dynamics of the social and
historical situation in which she finds herself. It is evident that
any attempt to represent experience, to reconstruct the past or
to confer identity necessarily draws on the resources of
memory and imagination, which recreate, sift and order the
writer's perceptions and experiences. In *Une femme*, the

narrator refers to the mythical dimension of her reconstruction of her mother's life (**23**), while Ernaux has said of her portrait of her father that 'la fiction passe où elle veut... *La Place* est de l'ordre du fictionnel dans la mesure où j'ai donné un destin à mon père'.[1] In considering the relationship between lived experience and its representation in Ernaux's writing, it is important for us to reflect on the status of the 'I' which is inscribed in the texts. The first-person narrative voice which recounts *La Place* and *Une femme* is not perceived by Ernaux as a voice which is hers alone, nor as a universal voice; rather it is a voice which articulates a specific social experience which is shared by many people. For Ernaux, the alienation which she feels as a result of her divided class identity is crucial to her practice as a writer. 'What can one write?' is inseparable from the nagging 'How does one write?'. The person who is in a state of internal exile, between two worlds, one where, as people say, you work with your hands, and the other where you work with your head, also feels caught between two languages: the loved, familiar idiom of books, the essential source of liberation, and the mother language, concrete, commonly spoken, expressing more than the other the relationship with what is real and the conditions of life. No matter how attached a writer may be to the first, he knows that it is not appropriate for him, any more than inherited literary forms such as the novel, whether it be traditional or 'new', and that conforming to these would be conforming with the dominant social and aesthetic order and denying himself all the more, himself and the world he came out of. He needs to seek his voice and his form, to express a reality which the writer of, let us for convenience say 'bourgeois' origins, has not the slightest inkling.

> For myself, this voice is founded on the 'I', not so much that this 'I' would be the depository for individuality, for a new and particular vision, but just the opposite, rather for a general experience, or at least for one shared in common by a great number of people.[2]

In *La Place* and *Une femme*, the narrator does not give herself a name and refers to her parents only as 'mon père' and 'ma mère'; their surnames are represented by a single letter (D...). Our analysis will also primarily identify the 'I' as 'the narrator', rather than as Ernaux; we hope that this will draw attention to what might be called the 'porosity' of the narrative

'I', while also encouraging readers to reflect critically on the perennially complex question of the relationship between author and narrator. Even if an author apparently speaks 'directly' through a given text, it is with a voice that can only partially and imperfectly illuminate the necessarily Protean subjectivity from which it issues.

Since we first began to work on *La Place* and *Une femme*, we have been concerned to address the following question: given the predominantly youthful readership anticipated for this series, what would be the main appeal of Ernaux's texts? At first sight, the themes of *La Place* and *Une femme* make the texts a less than obvious choice for presentation to sixth-formers and undergraduates: written as a response to the death of a father, then a mother—delayed by some fifteen years in the case of *La Place*, more or less immediate in the case of *Une femme*—and conceived in part as a selective family history from the 1890s to the 1980s, it might seem that their primary appeal would be to readers in their middle years. Such readers are more likely to have to come to terms with the death of parents, and, for a variety of reasons (for example a desire to establish continuity in the face of death and to hold on to what has been lost or may soon be lost) to be interested in preserving the memory of the daily existence of their immediate forebears. Evidently, death is an ever-present threat, even to the very young, and although it is not common for the death of a parent to occur at this time in their lives, they frequently have to deal with the loss of grandparents and with the difficulties and adjustments which bereavement often provokes. However, it may be argued that *La Place* and *Une femme* centre less on bereavement in itself than on the narrator's desire to explore and assess her relationship with her parents, to situate herself in relation to their background, aspirations and achievements. Adolescents and young adults need to establish a sense of autonomous identity, to work towards self-definition, or at least to sketch in the parameters of what they might become; for most adolescents, this involves measuring themselves against their parents, instinctively assessing how far and in what ways their parents' values, norms and achievements match or run counter to their own aspirations. Inevitably, the feelings of a teenager or young adult towards his or her parents (probably still relatively young, with years of active life ahead of them) will be very different from those of a mature person towards their elderly or deceased parents, but in both cases the parent-child connection is likely to generate ambivalent and painful emotions which often remain unspoken, perhaps even unacknowledged.

Here we touch upon a fundamental aspect of Ernaux's practice as a writer: her concern to explore areas of experience which are normally excluded from the public domain. Ernaux frequently aligns writing with transgression, the breaking of a taboo: 'pour moi, l'écriture a eu toujours un petit peu cette fonction de dire ce que l'on sent mais sans oser le dire, de libérer des choses qui sont très refoulées dans les gens, très au fond d'eux-mêmes et qui ne se disent pas'.[3] This determination to articulate what normally remains unsaid manifests itself in *La Place* and *Une femme* in several ways. Most obviously, the narrator's apparently matter-of-fact dissection of her relationship with her parents may shock or disturb readers who prefer not to look beneath the surface of their own filial feelings. The frank evocation of caring for a victim of Alzheimer's disease, the unblinking account of her mother's progressive deterioration and the resolutely factual description of the everyday routine of a residential home also broach a realm which is commonly experienced, but rarely articulated. Ernaux's desire to explore the meaning of bereavement, and to expose the hierarchical class system which structures contemporary French society, provides further examples of this determination to open up areas of experience which too often are passed over in silence as we attempt to paper over the cracks which threaten the comfortable stability of our existence.

To conclude this brief introduction to our study of *La Place* and *Une femme*, it seems appropriate to comment on the kind of reading which we have undertaken. The style of both works appears at first to be straightforward, the themes and meaning of the text readily accessible. However, those who approach the texts more attentively will quickly discover that, for all its directness, Ernaux's taut prose makes considerable demands on the reader. The predominance of unelaborated concrete detail, together with the frequent breaks in the text and the absence of transitional comment, gives the text a notational quality which leaves maximum space for interpretation: readers are likely to be drawn into a complex network of associations and ideas owing as much to their own experience and awareness as to Ernaux's. The tight connection between concentrated analysis of feeling and writing in the composition of *La Place* and *Une femme*, and the author's determination to identify and communicate only what is essential, result in a dense style in which each word is charged with meaning. The reader's active participation is further invited by Ernaux's refusal to offer a conventional way of interpreting her parents' experience, as she could have done, for example, by stressing the picturesque elements of their youthful existence or by depicting them in a way likely to engage the reader's sympathy; instead, she keeps her readers at a distance from the lives she describes, obliging us to recognize the specificity of her parents' existence and to acknowledge the reality of social difference. Our main priority, in analysing *La Place* and *Une femme*, will be to draw out some of the assumptions, implications and connections which underlie these very concentrated texts, so that readers are in a better position constructively to address the questions raised by Ernaux's work and to elaborate their own diverse responses to it.

NOTES

(1)   Reported by Jean-Jacques Gibert in 'Le Silence ou la Trahison?', *Révolution*, 260, 22 février 1988.

(2)   From a statement which Ernaux wrote for the issue of *The Review of Contemporary Fiction* entitled 'New French Fiction' (vol. IX, Spring 1989), pp. 210-11 (translation by Dominic D. Bernadi).

(3)   Talk at Winchester College, 10 March 1988. We are indebted to Alan Conn, Head of Modern Languages at Winchester College, for making available to us a recording of Ernaux's talk.

La Place

La Place has, at first glance, an air of simplicity: a straightforward narrative line; a language that is simple and direct; a style that is economical and uncluttered. Closer inspection, however, reveals a work of considerable subtlety which operates on a number of levels. One immediately striking feature of the text is the incorporation of a sequence of autoreferential passages which punctuate the narrative at regular intervals, and which form a running commentary on its creation, its aims and progress, and the difficulties encountered. Such interventions, in foregrounding the mechanisms of writing, take us beyond the ostensible surface of the narrative—the story of a life—and place before our attention issues of a broader nature: the relationship between the narrator and her material; the question of distance and involvement; the motivations which underlie the writing of the text; the status and function of literature. All these point us towards an important preliminary question: how is the reader to address this work?

The question of how to situate and classify the narrative in relation to established literary genres is not confronted as squarely in *La Place* as it will be in *Une femme.* Nevertheless there are points where the text signals, directly or indirectly, what it strives not to be. To begin with, we can observe that it strives not to be, in any fully fledged sense of the term, a biography. Nowhere do we find the exhaustive documentation or the accumulated minutiae of daily existence that are normally associated with this kind of literary project. On the contrary, this is a spare and episodic text, ruled throughout by a principle of rigorous selectivity. There are both drastic telescopings (for example, the father's activities against the five-year backcloth of World War Two are related in a page and a half), and silences: we see relatively little of the relationship between husband and wife.

Nor does the text display that concern for chronological precision which is the usual marker of the biographical enterprise. Although dates do figure from time to time, very often the reader must decode and situate glancing cultural references: the fashion for short skirts and cropped hair denoting the 1920s; the advent of television, the 1950s; the appearance of the first supermarket, the 1960s. Alternatively, we have to piece together snippets of information, relating for example a wholly indeterminate 'À cette époque' to the fact that the narrator is having her first periods (**82**). Indeed there are moments when the chronology remains purposefully opaque, as in the section recounting the occasion when the narrator first takes home her middle-class prospective husband, a manifestly memorable event for all concerned which is introduced with the vague 'À la fin d'un été' (**94**). What motivates this narration is clearly not a desire to chart fully and accurately the day-to-day experience of a given individual.

Nor, it may be added here, does the text seek to present itself as an exercise in private nostalgia, an attempt to 'bring back to life' times past and persons departed. The narrator explicitly rejects 'la poésie du souvenir' (**24**) and sets her text firmly apart from the strategies of 'evocative' literary description. A brief, ironic foray into the supposed rustic charms of peasant life, complete with touches of local colour and regional vocabulary, is curtly dismissed with the comment 'Ce serait facile de faire quelque chose dans ce genre' (**33**). Later, the narrator underlines the unhelpful and unproductive nature of misty reminiscence: 'La couleur du ciel, les reflets des peupliers dans l'Oise toute proche, n'avaient rien à m'apprendre' (**100**). The narrator's concern lies with more tangible realities: what she seeks to record are words and gestures, 'les faits marquants' and 'les signes objectifs' (**24**).

Lastly, we should note that the text does not assume the status of a novel. Though Fernandez-Récatala (p. 169) uses the term for her seven works so far, the fact that (at Ernaux's own insistence) the work is not designated *roman* in her publisher's lists is an unobtrusive signal. More explicit is the revelation made early in *La Place* (**23-4**) that in the months following her father's death the narrator had begun a novel with her father as its central character. We might surmise that this enterprise was undertaken in response to an urge comparable to that which was later to fuel the composition of *Une femme:* the need to come to terms, through the medium of writing, with the immediate experience of bereavement. But the project was abandoned in disgust, and the narrator, embarking now on the composition of *La Place*, some fifteen years after her father's death, knows that 'le roman est impossible'. The reasoning behind this realisation, though articulated economically, is instructive. 'Le parti de l'art' which the narrator refuses to adopt seems to imply that the 'artistry' of novelistic techniques invariably carries with it an emotional or affective charge: such writing will ensnare the writer into revealing a set of subjective responses (regret, pity, scorn), and hence into adopting a position which is inevitably judgmental. As a consequence, the reader's sympathies or antipathies will be engaged and swayed by an 'angled' presentation. To avoid such responses, the narrator will employ what she terms 'l'écriture plate', or elsewhere in the text 'le ton du constat' (**89-90**): a discourse which seeks to remain on the even, dispassionate level of an official document; a register which aspires to be factual, neutral, non-judgmental, objective.

l'écriture plate

Now there are vexed issues involved here which require comment. Firstly, the very concept of 'objectivity' is perennially open to question.Any human being perceives and experiences the world through the filter of an individual consciousness, and it is legitimate to propose that each one of us interprets and understands those perceptions and that experience in a wholly personal fashion. However strenuously one might aspire to an 'objective' understanding, an element of subjectivity can, arguably, never be fully eliminated. Moreover, any attempt to give verbal expression to an experience inevitably entails a choice of terms and locutions; and language, however carefully it is deployed, has the power to betray underlying layers of private attitudes and responses. An obvious contemporary example of this lies in our growing awareness of how the most arid offical document can enshrine prejudice of a sexist nature. Whether language can ever be used in a truly 'neutral' fashion remains an open question. These are problems of which Ernaux is wholly aware, and we shall have cause to return to them at a later stage in this study.

The second issue concerns the status of any form of narrative. As Ernaux herself has recognised in an interview with the authors (July 1990), any attempt to narrate a sequence of events involves a process of manipulation. Decisions have to be taken concerning the selection of material to be presented, the order and the manner in which it is to be set forth. In a strict sense, any narrative will entail an element of 'storytelling' which imparts to the raw material narrated a degree of 'fictionality'. In Ernaux's own words, 'toute organisation est forcément de la fiction'. It follows therefore that the narrative strategies inherent in 'le parti de l'art' can never be wholly avoided: they can only be minimised.

It is in this more relativistic perspective that we should evaluate the narrator's choice of narrative technique. 'Le ton du constat' represents an attempt to present material in as neutral and as factual a fashion as is possible. In its essence, it takes the form of a series of direct notations, held apart from each other by blank expanses, and presented without a running commentary of analysis or personal response. It is a strategy which achieves several effects: it reflects the texture of the discourse in letters written by the narrator's own parents or relatives (important since, as already noted, the way individuals handle language is obliquely revelatory of their attitudes and values, their perceptions of themselves and of their position in the world); it enables the narrator to exploit the suggestive power of careful juxtapositions; it obliges the reader to respond to the text constructively, perceiving (or supplying) hidden connections; and it sets the text firmly apart from the usual sequential flow of fictional, novelistic narrative.

leur place

Thus far we have examined what *La Place* is not, and it is time to consider in a more positive light what it sets out to be and to do. One important first clue lies in the title itself. For although the text seeks ostensibly to trace the life of the narrator's father, the title draws our attention not, as we might perhaps expect, to an individual, but to a concept. The significance of this distinction is signposted by the narrator herself in a section (**45-6**) where she discloses a temptation that constantly threatens to throw her narration off course: the indulgence in detailed reminiscence, the evocation of telling moments which would illuminate 'la figure particulière' of her father, and help capture some essential characteristic of his being. For the narrator this is a snare, the 'piège de l'individuel' which she must actively resist. Whenever, in the process of writing, the portrait of the father threatens to become dominant, occupying the centre of the stage, her mind is swamped and she loses all sense of concern with 'tous les signes d'une condition partagée avec d'autres'. It is here, ultimately, that her primary objective lies: the depiction of a condition that is shared, the sets of circumstances, pressures and constraints that operate on whole sections of society, shaping attitudes and values, governing the quality of experience and life. This focus means that the status of the father in the narrative is delicately poised. He stands at the foreground of the narrative, yet he is not intended as the primary centre of attention. His importance does not lie in his uniqueness as a human being, as a complex bundle of quirks and foibles that make him different from anyone else. We might note here that the device of designating him only by the initials A... D... (21; 111) indicates a deliberate move to depersonalise him, to rob him of a mark of identity, and to set a distance between him and the reader. What makes him important is precisely the opposite: it is what he has in common with others that is the focus of interest. In the text he is a representative figure, distilling and crystallizing the experience of many.[1]

The title, then, by decentring the father as an individual, points us from the start towards the broader concept of *place*, whose significance here is best pinpointed by quoting the first two abstract senses given by *Le Petit Robert*: 'le fait d'être classé dans une catégorie; position, situation dans laquelle on se trouve'; and 'position, rang dans une hiérarchie'. On this level, the text can be said to have an underlying drive which we can conveniently term 'documentary' in that it seeks to set forth, as faithfully and as dispassionately as can be achieved, the realities of position and class and how they intersect with the texture of lived experience. In a radio interview ('France Culture', 21 June 1984) Ernaux said of her objectives in writing *La Place*: 'J'ai voulu travailler comme un ethnologue'. The urge to adopt the detached scientific standpoint of the social and cultural anthropologist sets the perspective and the tone of the project: it will be characterised by a conscious effort neither to glamorise nor to sentimentalise, nor indeed, at the opposite pole of response, to deride or patronise. In the narrator's own terminology, the writing of *La Place* is an act of 'réhabilitation' (54). The term is worth pausing on, for its connotations in French are not quite the same as those of the English 'rehabilitation'. The English carries a stronger moral charge, suggesting the rectification of wrongs, the erasing of slurs prejudicial to rights or reputation. The French implies rather a restoring of consideration to something that has been neglected, but that has not necessarily fallen into disrepute. It is to this first level that we now turn.

'La réhabilitation d'un mode de vie' (54)

The trajectory of the father's life is a particularly informative one in that its historical span covers a period of

profound social and economic change. At the beginning of the
twentieth century, France was among the least industrialised
and developed of European nations, and a great deal of
ground had to be covered at speed as it hauled itself into line
with its neighbours. The progressive transitions in the father's
life reflect this national process, and at the same time allow us
insight into the complex and conflictual interaction of different
layers of French society.

father's life + industrial-isation

The circumstances into which the father was born were not,
in one sense, exceptional. Statistics tell us that at the turn of
the century approximately half of the French population
worked in some capacity on the land. His own father, however,
was located at the lowest level of this agricultural work-force,
belonging to the class of landless farm-labourer rather than
that of land-owning peasantry (who may not have been rich,
but who were certainly not grindingly poor). It is a measure of
the changelessness of this way of life, and of the absence of
possibility of escape therefrom, that his father had spent his
entire working existence, from the age of eight onwards, as a
labourer. It was a harsh life that bred a hard man, short-
tempered at the best of times, and grimly so when
drunk.Unable to read or write as a result of inadequate
schooling (enforced no doubt by economic necessities requiring
him to earn his keep as soon as he was physically able), he
clearly perceived his own illiteracy with resentment, reacting
violently at the sight of any member of the family practising a
skill which he had never had the opportunity to acquire. As the
narrator observes, the setting of her father's early years was
more reminiscent of the Middle Ages than of the dawn of the
twentieth century.

(g-père)

At first it seemed likely that the son was destined to follow in
the father's footsteps. Schooling was interrupted by
absenteeism when he was needed to help with work on the
farm, and he in his turn was withdrawn from school before
gaining a qualification, in order to earn his keep. But he at least
had made a significant advance: he had learned to read and
write. This is an early pointer to a theme that is of major
importance in *La Place*: the role and value of education. We
shall be examining this issue in detail at a later stage. For the
moment we shall note simply that the father's literacy has
perhaps a greater significance than might at first be thought.
While it would be an overstatement to pretend that the ability
to read and write represented a magical key that would open

(le père)

all doors, it is fair to say that it was an enabling acquisition for the father, one which allowed at least the possibility of an escape route from the condition in which his own father had remained helplessly enclosed. Moreover, the father's awareness of the benefits of education would later play a crucial part in shaping his attitudes to the studies of his own child, thus contributing directly to the narrator's formation and development.

The first opportunity for such an escape, together with the urge to take advantage of it, arose as a result of intersecting events. The First World War had weakened the hold of tradition, particularly on the young. The narrator notes (34) how wine was now being drunk instead of cider, the staple drink of Normandy, and how farm boys were increasingly disdained by the village girls: signs it would seem of a growing sense of upward aspiration.The father's military service (which must have closely followed the end of the war) had taken him out of the closed village world and broadened his horizons: the experience of city life, travel, and the enforced class levelling of army existence left him determined not to return to agriculture. And the rapid industrialisation of France in the immediate post-war years provided the one way out: factory work.

This decisive move on the father's part is summed up by the narrator with the laconic comment 'Sorti du premier cercle' (35), implying the further transitions yet to come. But before turning to these, it is worth pausing to identify a theme which runs throughout *La Place*, and which is observed with particular sharpness: the relationship between occupation and social standing, and the hierarchical attitudes that this engenders. We have already noted the early signs of a disdain for country life and ways (the first stirrings, in fact, of what was to develop into a demographic sea-change: the so-called *exode rural* as the young in France increasingly fled the countryside for the towns and cities). Later in the text the narrator elaborates on this phenomenon. Those now living urban lives were at pains to conceal their rural origins.'Faire paysan' was to appear backward, behind the times, unsophisticated (70). The peasant was dumb, and an object of derision. But such sneering was not reserved solely for country folk.Similar divisions existed between different categories of urban workers.Factory girls were perceived as sluttish by those who were 'in service' in well-off households (36). By

etc
↑
factory workers
↑
peasants

implication, the status of male factory worker was no higher, since the narrator's mother was always proud to be able to say (though with dubious justification, perhaps?) «Mon mari n'a jamais fait ouvrier» (36). The picture we are given is of a highly stratified society, with each level ever mindful of its ranking in the hierarchy. So that while factory workers could deem themselves superior to the peasants, they themselves would be simultaneously aware of their own inferiority in the eyes of the layer immediately above. As we shall see, such a refined and intense degree of class-consciousness bred an atmosphere of permanent mistrust and insecurity. Along with the new mobility of postwar French society came a watchfulness and a hypersensitivity, where the supercilious glance of a town-centre saleswoman (90) could be experienced as paralysingly intimidating.

Against this background, the father's move to factory work in Y...² unquestionably represented an upward step. The accommodation he could now rent in the town, with its upstairs bedroom (a dream come true for his new wife), was a far cry from the single-storeyed thatched dwelling, with its floors of beaten earth, that he had known as a child. But it was at the same time a step into a different dimension of inferiority, and an awareness of a new set of prejudices bearing down from above. It is legitimate to wonder (even though the text does not make this point explicitly) to what extent these pressures fuelled the urge to leave manual work behind and to continue the ascent up the ladder. In fact the text suggests that it was a concern for her husband's safety following an accident (he had by now left the rope-making factory and was working as a roofer) that prompted the wife to suggest shopkeeping as an alternative way of earning a living. But it is interesting to note that in *Une femme* the role of social ambition is unequivocally stated. There we are told that the wife was 'fière d'être ouvrière mais pas au point de le rester toujours, rêvant de la seule aventure à sa mesure: prendre un commerce d'alimentation'. And the narrator adds that the wife was 'la volonté sociale du couple', and that the husband followed her dynamic lead (F, 39). There are moreover details in *La Place* which show how considerations of 'standing' were intimately bound up with this new business venture. The financial problems of the early years left them forever terrified that they might, in a revealing turn of phrase, 'retomber ouvriers' (39). Similarly, when the father was eventually driven to take another manual job in order to make ends meet, the narrator notes in a key passage recalling the title how 'Il cherchait à tenir sa place. Paraître plus commerçant qu'ouvrier' (45). The new status of *commerçant* was one to which they clung with a fierce pride.

Inevitably, however, the pride and sense of achievement were accompanied once again by a new network of constraints, and this time perhaps more delicately lethal than those they had known as factory workers. In a milieu already characterised by prying eyes and instant condemnatory judgements, their position in the *café-épicerie* was especially exposed and vulnerable. The 'regard critique' and the opinions of neighbours and customers were to be feared. Everything they said or did had to be carefully monitored, tailored to be as bland and inoffensive as possible. Their natural desire to keep up the appearances befitting their new status was constantly tempered by the fear of being judged arrogant or pretentious. Petty jealousy and treachery lay on all sides, not least in the bosom of their own immediate family, whose members could cheerfully avail themselves of the hospitality that the couple's (relative) prosperity made possible, while secretly despising them as 'riches' (45). In later years, as we shall see, the very fact of having an academically gifted child would be felt as a potential source of embarrassment, as though this constituted in the eyes of others an undeserved privilege, or evidence of an indecent ambitiousness on their part.

But there was worse. It was a disagreeable consequence of their move up the hierarchy that they were now economically dependent on a clientele that could easily take its custom elsewhere, should offence be given or feathers ruffled.[3] To be thus at the mercy of others was experienced with resentment, particularly by the father, and all the more so perhaps since their clientele, both at L... and subsequently at Y..., was drawn principally from the levels of society that they had succeeded in leaving behind. To his wariness and mistrust was added the feeling of hatred: not merely for the customers and the power they wielded, but also for himself and the servile stance which financial necessity forced him to adopt.

What needs to be stressed here is that the humiliation and the alienation which characterised the father's position were generated in the first place by a combination of social and economic pressures emanating from the broad sector of society to which he himself belonged. There is no attempt here to promote a myth of an amicable proletarian solidarity. On the contrary, his immediate milieu was one permanently preoccupied with status and rank, shot through with the envy and the back-biting that such rivalry breeds: a sector of society, in short, divided against itself.

Now *La Place* does not set out explicitly to explore the mechanisms of this phenomenon, or account for its origins. But as we have noted, Ernaux is a writer who manages to suggest much via careful juxtapositions, leaving the reader to establish parallels and connections which the text itself does not spell out. In this way it is possible that the text invites us to envisage an explanation by setting the portrait of a divided working class alongside the portrait of the greater divide which runs through French society: that separating 'la classe dominée' from 'la classe dominante'.[4]

For the father, the upper reaches of the social scale constituted a distant and intimidating world, with its own language, values and special codes of conduct, where it was all too easy to commit gaffes that would humiliatingly reveal the extent to which he was 'out of place'. It was a source of acute embarrassment and shame to be found travelling (although quite inadvertently) in a first-class railway carriage with a second-class ticket, to have written 'à prouver' instead of 'approuvé' on a legal document, or to be unfamiliar with the code of etiquette underlying the expression 'costume de ville' (60). While he prided himself on speaking standard French rather than the Norman dialect (which had been the sole mode of expression of his own parents), in reality it was only 'en partie' (62) that he had rid his language of *patois*. So that although he was very much aware of the importance of speech patterns as an indicator of social ranking, carefully monitoring his own language when in the presence of those who 'parlaient bien', it was inevitable that slips would occur to undermine the impression he was striving to give.

The measure of his exclusion from this other world was reflected too in more subtle ways, as in the delicate matters of taste and *savoir-vivre*. His modernisation of the café, entailing the covering-up of open fireplaces, exposed beams and the half-timbered façade, and the installation of neon strips, was to coincide almost exactly with the growing taste for cosy lamplight and period authenticity (compare pp. 57 and 84). And when the narrator brought home her university friends, his over-zealous attempts to dispense gracious hospitality

managed only to betray the social and cultural gulf separating him from these girls who had been 'si bien élevées' (92-3).

Consciousness of this gulf served in the first instance as a constant reminder of his own inferiority. But it also fostered a profound and generalised mistrust. Not only the government was seen as a hostile force, favouring the interests of big business to the detriment of the small shopkeeper. Even an innocent compliment on the period charm of their house (57) was construed as a cunning form of oppression, designed to keep them 'in their place' and contented with their lot, and thus to neutralise any aspirations to better things.

paranoia

What is interesting here is that the father's interaction with both the *classe dominée* and the *classe dominante* produces a near-identical set of responses: a sense of inferiority and exclusion; the feelings of resentment and suspicion. The humiliation he experiences in the presence of those located in the higher levels is matched by that engendered by the deferential attitude he must assume for his clientele. The belief that in either domain no-one can be trusted is developed almost to the point of paranoia: 'Le monde entier ligué' (75). It is possible that this parallelism suggests that there is a causal connexion between the basic division of French society into a dominant class and a dominated class, and the internal divisiveness which permeates the latter. In other words, that the members of the *classe dominée* are so suffused by the sense of inferiority imposed from above that they re-enact within their own sphere the strategies of oppression that are exercised against them. Unable to evade a dominant judgment that classifies them as mediocre and second-rate, they seek compensation by establishing a hierarchical structure of their own within which they can jockey and vie with each other for a kind of position and rank.

classe dominant
↓
classe dominée
↓
others

We must stress again that this is not a view that is articulated in *La Place*; it is an inference we have drawn from an interesting parallelism in the text. That said, the same parallelism leads us to a further conclusion that can be advanced with more certainty. In the father's dealings with both sectors of society there exists another striking common denominator: that of dissimulation. Contact with those who were perceived to belong to the *classe dominante* called for a donning of clothes, the adoption of an etiquette and a register of speech that did not come naturally, but that were deemed 'suitable'. That in itself is not surprising. More arresting is the fact that his dealings with those from his own immediate social context demanded a comparable degree of concealment. Business sense required that personal views, especially concerning political issues, remain well hidden: 'Il gardait ses idées pour lui.*Il n'en faut pas dans le commerce*' (**42**). Worse still, not merely opinions but material facts had to be judiciously filtered. An excellent example of the tightrope that peer pressure forced him to walk concerns the narrator's own studies. To have a daughter at university exposed him to the damning charge of being rich. On the other hand, to reveal that she was a *boursière* in receipt of a grant exposed him to the charge of being excessively lucky to have a child who was paid by the state to 'do nothing' (**91-2**). Forever caught between two sets of constraints, the father must on one side disguise his perceived inferiority, and on the other conceal his perceived privilege. The narrator notes that the hallmarks of her father's life were 'solitude' and 'méfiance' (**42**). To those we could add a third: the enforced need to live a false existence.

The insistence on these pressures certainly fulfils the narrator's avowed aim (**54-5**) of denouncing the alienation that characterised her father's condition. But the equal and parallel aim of giving expression to the happiness that such a life afforded is perhaps less fully realised. For while the trajectory of the father's life is in a sense a success story, and while he and his wife could take justifiable pride in the tangible evidence of their achievement (they possessed a car, and owned their property), it has to be recognised that the explicit references to happiness in the text are not overly compelling. Most seem to be phrased in a way that skirts unequivocal affirmation. The couple's own summing-up of the early years of their business venture reads «*Il y avait plus malheureux que nous*» (**44**). The narrator notes that her father 'paraissait heureux' (**65**) while driving through the countryside listening to popular music. Later we are told that 'il n'était pas malheureux' (**76**), and that the couple believed that '*on ne peut pas être plus heureux qu'on est*' (**77**).[5] These faint qualifications and negative formulations cast a shadow of doubt, as though the evidence she is able to muster leaves the narrator somewhat less than convinced. Indeed, late on in the text, as she feels her narration drawing to a close, she comments that she cannot now go back over what she has written to add or modify details, or to wonder 'où était le bonheur' (**101**). An admission, it would seem, that the quest to 'dire le bonheur' has met with doubtful success. The reader is left to ponder a dangling question: was there a happiness that was in fact felt, but that the narrator has failed to articulate because her twin aims ('dire à la fois le bonheur et l'aliénation') are irreconcilably contradictory? Or was the happiness never there in the first place?

On balance, it has to be said that the text lays more emphasis on the forces that oppress than on those that liberate. Even though the father lived through a period marked by a new degree of social mobility, and was able to take advantage of the possibilities of betterment thus afforded, the space in which he could manoeuvre remained sharply circumscribed. An unbridgeable cultural gap excluded him from accession to the *classe dominante*, breeding a sense of resignation, an acceptance of inferiority. And within the inescapable framework of the *classe dominée* he was trapped by a system which contrived simultaneously to despise inferiority and to condemn what it saw as excessive ambition. The very concept of *place*, entailing classification within or against a hierarchy, imposed the daily awareness of boundaries and barriers beyond which it was either impossible, or dangerous, to pass. In a way, it comes as no surprise for us to be told that 'Il ne rit sur aucune photo' (56).

Within the context of the 'réhabilitation d'un mode de vie' the narrator's overriding purpose is to give expression to what she terms elsewhere in the text (101) 'la réalité oubliée' of her father's social and cultural experience. The phrase is telling. If the realities of life experienced by the father and those of his class have been 'forgotten', it is in obedience to a dominant ideology which deems this particular dimension of human reality inferior, unlovely, and best left in decent oblivion. It is a cultural veto which the narrator had discovered at school, where she was prevented from drawing on her immediate experience of her own home life for her essays. The material was not 'suitable'. The *classe dominante* decrees that 'les souvenirs du monde d'en bas' must be suppressed. They are 'de mauvais goût' (73). *La Place* seeks to transgress this veto. Unflinchingly the text lays before us not merely a set of social circumstances, but an array of personal details concerning her father's attitudes and behaviour: speech patterns, prejudices, eating habits, hygiene, even his taste for pornographic books (78). Ernaux has reported that some readers have expressed surprise at such openness, regarding the exposure of such

taboo subjects discussed

intimate matters as tantamount to a breach of family confidence. It is an over-squeamish and inappropriate reaction, for the candour is essential to the project of laying bare that which the dictates of 'good taste' aim to suppress, of speaking the unspeakable. And the flat matter-of-factness of the presentation is designed to elicit from the reader a more detached response: the reality which the text depicts is a phenomenon which exists, and which is worthy not only of our attention but of our serious consideration and understanding.

But there is another dimension to *La Place* which takes us beyond the 'réhabilitation d'un mode de vie', and where the documentary thrust is intersected by a current of profound personal involvement. For there is an obvious sense, as we noted earlier, in which the text can be perceived as inherently subjective, despite its determination to aspire to detachment and objectivity. As Ernaux herself has readily acknowledged to us, the material contained in *La Place* has been experienced, and is recounted, 'par une subjectivité'—in other words, her own. That fact is inescapable. But there is a more important way in which the carefully dispassionate narrative stance becomes enmeshed with a perspective which is overtly subjective. Within the text the concept of place is widened to encompass the narrator's own mobile position within the social hierarchy. A new set of issues is thus brought into play: the relationship between the narrator and her origins; between herself and her family; even, we might say, between herself and herself. Here we must confront a complementary aim underpinning the writing of *La Place*:the desire to give expression to the narrator's migration from one class to another, to explore and to explain the rift that was thus opened up between father and daughter.

'Une distance de classe [...] qui n'a pas de nom' (23)

The obvious point of entry into this dimension of *La Place* is the theme of education, which interconnects with the issues of position and class on a number of important levels. As we have already had occasion to note, the father was very conscious of education as an enabling acquisition. Indeed, it is suggested that this awareness was instilled in him from an early age, when his own schoolmaster would berate him and his brother for missing school with the words «Vos parents veulent donc que vous soyez misérables comme eux!» (29). Even though he visualised the world of education (much as he did the world of the bourgeoisie) as something distant and awesome, where he had no part to play, and even though he was unable to comprehend the idea that study could be in itself an enjoyable activity, rather than a necessary but disagreeable stepping stone, he was from the start to encourage his daughter's abilities. He had faith that academic achievement would bring social betterment, in short, that she would end up '*mieux que lui*' (74). Events were to prove him right, and the pride he took in her success is graphically embodied in the contents of his wallet which the narrator empties after his death: an old photograph of himself as a manual worker is enclosed within a newspaper cutting listing his daughter's name as having come second in the competitive examination for entry into the *école normale d'institutrices* (the training college for primary school teachers). It is a potent image, summing up the enormous advance made in the space of a generation.

But the advance came at a price. Or more precisely, a series of prices. To begin with, the very knowledge that the narrator acquired at school came to provoke family rows as she criticised her father's standards of hygiene, his eating habits or the quality of his language. A distance opened between them. Now this was no doubt, in part, a normal process of teenage rebellion. But the shaping processes of her education contributed in a major way to the growing rift.[6] She became increasingly aware of his inability to think independently, to reason and argue. The more she penetrated into the world of literature and ideas, the more sharply she perceived his indifference to culture, and indeed to her own studies—for while he was pleased that she should study, the nature and content of the study were of no interest to him. They had nothing in common, no ground on which to make contact and communicate.

This estrangement was compounded by the social mobility which her intelligence made possible. As a bright and able girl she was invited to the homes of her middle-class schoolfriends. The new environment seemed everything that her father's was not: graceful and urbane; literate and witty; eminently 'civilised'. It was a world that seemed more in tune with her own developing interests and ideas, and its values and attitudes came, gradually but inexorably, to be her own.

Viewing her father from the other side of the class divide, she saw him anew: 'Mon père est entré dans la catégorie des gens simples ou modestes ou braves gens' (80).

We must pause here, for the preceding citation raises two interesting issues. We should note firstly that the narrator here is deploying in relation to the bourgeoisie the same technique she used when evoking the speech patterns of her parents. The italicisation of words and expressions serves to hold them up for our inspection, inviting us to consider how certain locutions reveal an inner world of values and attitudes. In this case, the apparently courteous adjectives used by the middle class to designate the lower classes reveal precisely what they are designed to conceal: an immense, patronising condescension. A comparable example is found in the section where the narrator takes home her middle-class university friends. Even though they were selected with care for their avowed lack of prejudice, they nevertheless betray their perception of the father's inferiority, and a condescending attitude towards him, by addressing him in a register of popular speech ('comme ça va-ti?')[7]

The second issue raised here concerns the position of the narrator herself in relation to the material she sets before us. For although in *La Place* the narrator charts her progressive integration into the world of the educated, professional middle class, she also sets up a distance between herself and her adopted milieu. Indeed it is fair to say that throughout the text her presentation of the middle class is shot through with a discreet irony. The teenager may have been captivated by the seeming elegance of this other world; the mature narrator is less mesmerised. Recalling how impressed she had been in her youth by the politeness, the niceness, and the apparently genuine concern for one's welfare manifested by 'des personnes bien éduquées' (72), the narrator observes drily that she was later to realise how hollow these mannerisms really were. In the section recounting the occasion when her future husband first visited her home (94), she notes how her parents unquestioningly assumed that to come from a 'good' background was an automatic guarantee of moral worth. It is hard to resist the unspoken implication that the belief was not well founded. In a similar vein, her brief evocations of the life style espoused on her marriage (hessian-covered walls, antiques, whisky as an aperitif) suggest that these were not the emblems of an individualistic, creative tastefulness; rather they

the m.c

stand as an alternative set of standardised and clichéd cultural markers.

What needs to be stressed here is the careful construction of narrative stance. The dispassionate approach which characterises the narrator's portrayal of her parents' world is counterbalanced by ironic distance in the evocation of the world of the middle class. The mode of narration seems itself to indicate that the narrator situates herself in neither domain, but remains apart from both. Further evidence of this can be seen at certain moments in the text where the narrator sets up sharp contrasts in cultural attitudes, but refuses to pass a value judgment of any kind. Noting the fact that financial constraints meant that her mother could afford to close the café only for an hour to accommodate her husband's funeral, the narrator observes that such behaviour is at odds with 'une vision distinguée du monde' (17), where silence and dignity would be the order of the day.Later she notes that a photograph of her father taken in the yard shows the outdoor lavatory and wash-house; details which 'un œil petit-bourgeois n'aurait pas choisis comme fond' (47). But in each case the narrator does no more than identify cultural differences, and refuses to align herself with one side or another. For the moment we merely signpost this phenomenon, for we shall need to examine it in more detail, and in the light of further information, at a later stage.

Returning to the issue of education, the essential point to be made is that it is presented in *La Place* as having, for those located in the lower layers of the social hierarchy, both a positive and a negative pole. It is on the one hand an acquisition, permitting social and financial betterment, the access to culture and power;[8] but on the other it can incur estrangement, separation and loss. The distance between father and daughter that is opened up during her school years is progressively widened by the wedge of her continuing education. Already as a schoolgirl she came to perceive all the markers of her class and family environment as alien: taste, values, mannerisms, language. Once she has left home, obtained a degree, and married a middle-class husband, the gulf is all but unbridgeable. From within the milieu which she now inhabits, with its concern for tasteful interiors, its appreciation of classical music and antiques, her origins seem so remote as to become almost hypothetical: 'J'ai glissé dans cette moitié du monde pour laquelle l'autre n'est qu'un décor'

(96). From now on, each (infrequent) visit to her parents is experienced as an abrupt and startling confrontation with a raw reality which her mind had unobtrusively softened and remodelled along more graceful lines: a sharp reminder of the distance lying between them.

At intermittent moments in the text, this distancing is, by suggestion and association, perceived as an act of betrayal and consequently as a source of guilt. The account of the family rows provoked by the narrator's teenage criticisms of her father ends with a self-critical proposition: 'Il aurait peut-être préféré avoir une autre fille' (82). The idea is not pursued, but the comment in itself says much. To take the father to task for the habits of a lifetime appears, in retrospect, tantamount to a denigration, if not a rejection, of all that he stood for. In the name of a set of values, newly- acquired and deemed to be superior, the child scorns the environment (and by extension the class) into which she was born, and the standards which have presided over her upbringing. It is a reaction which many a teenager in comparable circumstances will have experienced, though few perhaps would willingly confront it squarely and recognise it for what it is: an act of treachery. The narrator, however, is unflinching in her self-portrait; in wondering whether the father might not have preferred a different child (by implication, one less ungrateful and disloyal), she acknowledges the transgression, and the hurt that may have been inflicted.[9]

There is an underlying link between this passage and an episode related a few pages later. Returning from a summer away from her parents, the narrator rediscovers them with a sharpened awareness of details that proclaim their status: the loud and quarrelsome nature of their speech; the uncertainty of country folk having to navigate their way out of town (the event probably takes place in Rouen); her father's red ears and mottled skin. At which point the narration makes an unexpected moral leap: 'Je ne me sentais plus le droit d'entrer à l'Université' (86). The connexion is for us to supply; and the clearest inference to be drawn is that the move into the youthful, seemingly unfettered and privileged realm of higher education suddenly appears as an attractive but unworthy escape route from her parents and their shuttered world. In other words, a betrayal of duty and allegiance.

We can cite, too, the opening section of the text, where the narrator's successful passage through the practical section of her teaching diploma examination inspires not the mingled sensations of joy and relief, as we might expect, but the feelings of anger and shame. It is as though the success marks an official ratification of her entry into that other world, a public recognition of her acceptability as a member of a superior caste,[10] and a tacit annihilation of her origins.

Finally, we must examine a statement which the text makes no attempt to foreground, but whose implications are considerable. On the occasion of her final visit to her parents, accompanied this time by her son, the narrator refers to their first evening together as 'Un beau soir calme, un moment qui ressemblait à un rachat' (103). In its theological sense the term is a powerful one. If the concept of atonement is to be evoked, then there has to be a transgression which precedes it. Once again it is for us to deduce the nature of the transgression. Here, it would seem, the sense of a harmonious family unit momentarily redeems the rupture which she has brought about through her migration to another class.

These oblique and laconic allusions to an undercurrent of guilt point to a new level of significance in *La Place*, and invite a modified reading of the text, and of the motivation which underlies it.

'Écrire c'est le dernier recours quand on a trahi' (9)

It is in this perspective that the point of the epigraph (taken from a televised interview with Genet in 1982) becomes fully clear. As we have seen, the documentary purpose of *La Place* is to write the 'réalité oubliée' of the father's social condition, and thus to bring it out of oblivion and into the public domain. We have also seen that the screen of decent silence which has concealed it has been erected in response to the dominant demands of middle-class taste. The awkward fact remains, however, that it is precisely to the *classe dominante* that the narrator herself migrated. And she too deferred to this cultural veto, in that she came to 'forget' her origins. Indeed, it was just that which allowed her to slip so easily into another class, as she explicitly recognises. In her own words, the bourgeois world 'm'était ouvert parce que j'avais oublié les manières, les idées et les goûts du mien' (93).

We should stress here that this 'forgetting' does not arise as

m.c made the w.c hide themselves

the result of some involuntary and inescapable process of the deficient human memory, but denotes a conscious wish to repress the unpalatable. Nowhere is this clearer than in the narrator's perception of her parents. Away from them, she visualised them not as they were, but in a purged and idealised form, as 'des corps glorieux' (97), a powerful theological expression denoting the beatific state of the chosen few. Her mind discreetly erased the features which (to a bourgeois eye) seem common and vulgar, in effect refashioning the father and mother into the parents she would have liked to have. The insidious power of this impulse to suppress the real is tellingly epitomized in the 'scène du mauvais cadeau' (98). To offer the father aftershave seems so wildly inappropriate that we are invited to wonder what could have prompted the choice. Is it possible that the idealised image of the father had so successfully supplanted the real in the narrator's mind that she genuinely considered this a suitable present to give? Or did the choice betray the desire to transform the father, encouraging him to acquire 'civilised' tastes which he did not naturally possess? From the text, the second seems the more likely ('Mon envie de pleurer comme autrefois «il ne changera donc jamais!»'), but whichever interpretation we choose we are led to the same unavoidable conclusion: the father was what he was, and the daughter would rather he were different. We are reminded of a fragment presented to us a few pages earlier: 'Un jour, avec un regard fier: «Je ne t'ai jamais fait honte»' (93). No commentary is offered on the father's words. But the surrounding evidence set before us inclines us to wonder how far he was right. There is a sense in which the narrator became contaminated by the values of the class she had entered, leading her to disown her past, and to construct an imaginary set of parents of a more refined and seemly kind, who would blend more harmoniously with the world into which she had moved.

The delicacy of this position lends a new edge to the text. We might legitimately wonder whether the urge to document the conditions of existence of a broad sector of society is in fact fuelled in the first place by a private sense of guilt and a desire to make amends. Viewed in this perspective, the writing of *La Place* as an act of 'réhabilitation' is also, in more than one way, an act of atonement. Indeed the text itself testifies thereto, intermittently, and in its characteristically understated fashion.Towards the end of her narration, the narrator

observes: 'J'ai fini de mettre au jour l'héritage culturel que j'ai
dû déposer au seuil du monde bourgeois et cultivé quand j'y
suis entrée' (**111**). Though she herself had disdained and
rejected her own class, she now refuses to connive in the
tasteful middle-class obliteration of her working-class origins,
and holds up her background for what it properly is: a cultural
inheritance that is in no way shameful. It is different; but it is
not inferior.

ironic,
considering
she no
longer
belongs
to it

On another level the text perhaps seeks also to make
amends for the distance which had increasingly separated her
from her father. The section of narrative dealing with the early
stages of the rift is concluded with an arresting hypothesis:
'J'écris peut-être parce qu'on n'avait plus rien à se dire' (**84**). As
usual, the proposition is not pursued. But the implications are
far-reaching, positing another dimension of motivation
underlying *La Place:* the writing of the text is an attempt to
construct a bridge that will, retrospectively, reconnect father
and daughter, and re-establish a dialogue.

On a further level still, we might suggest that the text also
seeks to repair an internal division in the narrator's own sense
of selfhood. Recalling how, on her visits home, she
'rediscovered' the all but forgotten reality of her parents'
manner and behaviour, the narrator notes that her awareness
of the gulf lying between herself and them brought with it a
sensation of inner estrangement: 'Je me sentais séparée de
moi-même' (**98**). There is a recognition here that the
environment in which she had been raised constitutes a reality
of which she is inescapably a product. To have forgotten it is
tantamount to a denial of an essential element of the self. This
explicit realisation sheds a retrospective light on earlier
moments in the text where the narrator underlines the fact that
the shaping conditions of her father's life were also the
conditions of her own (see pp. **24** and **46**). In this perspective
one could argue that the recreation of the father's world is
simultaneously an affirmation of the narrator's own roots.
There is an important analogy to be drawn here. In order to
reconstruct the reality of her father's experience, the narrator
goes back to his childhood, for the circumstances of his
upbringing constitute an essential factor in an understanding
of him. Indeed, the text makes the explicit point that for all his
status of *commerçant*, he was still in an important respect 'un
homme de la campagne' (**67**). In a directly comparable way, the
narrator herself is the complex product of differing

they are
more
similar
than they
realise

environments and cultural values, and their dynamic interaction. Here we would recall the point made earlier concerning the careful narrative stance in *La Place*, where the strategy of distancing implies that the narrator does not locate herself wholly in either class. We might suggest now that in writing *La Place*, the narrator charts the contours of the different worlds which have shaped her, and by setting them together in the space of a unified text, seeks to bring a sense of synthesis and integration to what had previously been experienced as irreconcilable difference and division.

to integrate the 2 worlds
she is a product of them both.

It remains to be asked just how successful these efforts towards reconciliation can be. In the early stages of the text the narrator recounts how, as she left Y... after her father's funeral(travelling, significantly, in a first-class compartment), two sudden thoughts came to her: '«maintenant, je suis vraiment une bourgeoise» et «il est trop tard»' (**23**). Too late for what? We are not told, but we might surmise that the narrator here evokes a not uncommon experience for the recently bereaved: the awareness of things left undone and unsaid, which could have been (or should have been) said and done, but for which there is no longer any opportunity. The juxtaposition of this feeling with the affirmation of middle-class status leads us to infer a preoccupation with class division, separation and distance, and the consciousness that death has set its seal of permanence on the gap. The text, however, continues immediately with a reference to the early and abandoned novel ('«il faudra que j'explique tout cela»'), with the implication that writing can, perhaps, in some way and in some measure transcend distance and loss. The novel, as we know, failed to meet this objective. But can *La Place* be seen as succeeding where the novel failed?

It has to be said immediately that the framing sections which open and close the text, and thereby occupy positions of prominence, focus our attention on cultural difference rather than on any form of reintegration. We have already noted that the Capes episode leaves the narrator filled with anger and shame. The stark juxtaposition of this section with that which follows ('Mon père est mort deux mois après') implies a hidden connecting link between the two, and the fact that her mind

often confuses the chronological sequence of the two events
reinforces this impression. The link perhaps is that, on the one
hand, both represent definitive moments of accession to a new
mode of being: entry into a professional world, and entry into a
kind of symbolic adulthood (the narrator later recalls how in
the days following her father's death the thought 'je suis une
grande personne' often came into her mind). On the other
hand, both events mark moments of separation and loss.

The issues of education and class come to the fore again in
the closing pages, and here in a highly dense and complex
fashion. The text consists of a series of fragments which are
chronologically jumbled, covering a time span which reaches
from the narrator's childhood to the immediate moment of
writing, and which are seemingly unrelated. They are,
however, interconnected by a subtle network of associations
which, in the manner of a musical coda, re-echo the major
themes of the entire work. The world of learning is represented
by the municipal library, where comparisons with church
suggest that this is a sacred domain whose mysteries are, for
both father and (at this stage) daughter, unfamiliar. The
memory of the father taking the narrator to school on his
bicycle calls forth the image of the father as a 'passeur entre
deux rives': a ferryman transporting the child from one world
to another, but not himself entering the realm where learning is
dispensed. It is perhaps this notion of a territory to which he
has no access which evokes the memory of the text
L'Expérience des limites, which itself recalls an expression used
earlier in the text: 'les limites [...] du monde où vécut mon père,
où j'ai vécu aussi' (46). We are not given the reason why the
narrator found the book disappointing from the start; but we
might draw the inference that she had hoped for a work which
would deal with the material realities of a certain social
condition, not one (in all probability) focused on the abstract
complexities of literary theory.[11] The distance between these
two areas of concern is restated in the fragment where the
narrator sets her activity as writer of *La Place* against her
professional duties as a teacher: the manipulation of ideas
involved in the second seems, against the realities of lived
experience which *La Place* seeks to recapture, an airy, cerebral
luxury which is distressingly divorced from the real.

The emphasis here is on the positive and negative aspects of
education: accession and exclusion, acquisition and loss. But
what is the alternative? The supermarket episode which closes

the text points to the consequences of failure to ascend the educational ladder. The checkout girl, who did not complete a successful passage through technical college, is caught in a dully repetitive round. And there is perhaps a discreet link here with the image of the father as ferryman, and with the words of the popular song he used to sing: '*C'est l'aviron qui nous mène en rond*'. The oarsman makes no progress: he merely goes round in circles.

Stagnation, or progress at a price. The alternatives are sharply crystallized in this closing section where the narrator notes the bitter irony of both her own and her father's position: 'Peut-être sa plus grande fierté, ou même, la justification de son existence: que j'appartienne au monde qui l'avait dédaigné'. He himself, by encouraging her studies, helped to engineer the estrangement which would inevitably ensue. Did he himself perceive the irony? The chilling possibility, with the conflicting emotions it might engender in the father's attitude to his daughter's success, is fleetingly contemplated earlier in the text: 'Et toujours la peur OU PEUT-ÊTRE LE DÉSIR que je n'y arrive pas' (**80**).

Given this constant emphasis on separation, is there any fashion in which the gap can be said to be bridged? Indeed, must we not recognise that in any literal sense, reconciliation cannot be achieved? *La Place* is a literary construct; it is not the stuff of reality itself. However faithfully or honestly writing may seek to reflect the texture of the real, the fact remains that it will always be a reflection. Whatever complex relationships may be said to exist between literature and reality, they can only ever be of a representational or symbolic kind. Within this strict perspective we must accept that whatever the narrator entered into the pages of *La Place*, the text could never alter the material reality of her migration to another class, or close the distance thus opened up between herself and her father, or herself and her origins.

But it is perhaps on the symbolic level that *La Place* may be said to succeed in constructing a bridge of a kind. The Genet epigraph acknowledges that writing is a last resort. But as Ernaux herself has observed in an interview, it is 'un recours quand même. C'est mieux que le silence'.[12] The primary achievement of *La Place* is to break the middle-class conspiracy of silence and to set forth, without glamorisation or sentimentalisation, the conditions and quality of a lower-class existence, and in so doing the text restores to it a dignity and a

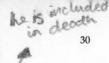

he is included in death

she gives her father culture + discussion by the bourgeoisie

value. But also, and more importantly, in writing her father's life the narrator in effect shifts that life into another realm: the realm of culture from which in real terms he had been forever excluded. The text brings about a symbolic migration whereby the father can enter the world into which the narrator has moved. It is worth noting too that in the same interview Ernaux conceded the point that, although the text strives to present the father as a representative rather than an individual figure, he nevertheless emerges as 'une espèce de héros de roman'. In that sense too he acquires, through the medium of literature, a status denied him in life: he is, we might say, 'written into the world'.

At this concluding juncture it is legitimate to point out that, on a personal level, Ernaux herself regards the text as having constructed a positive and lasting bridge. In the interview referred to above she identifies an important difference which sets *La Place* apart from her preceding first-person narratives. In this work, the narrating 'I' goes beyond the isolated world of interior monologue and establishes dialogue: 'Le «je» qui s'y trouve encore dialogue déjà avec un «il»—la vie de mon père—et ce «je» ne sera, je le crois, plus jamais seul'. A contact has been established, a degree of reconciliation achieved.

We would end by suggesting that this element of positive achievement is perhaps conveyed (albeit in a highly oblique manner) within the pages of *La Place* itself. At the very start of the narrative, where the moment of the father's death is recounted for the first time, the narrator recalls her mother descending the stairs to break the news: 'Elle a dit d'une voix neutre: «C'est fini»' (13). Much later, however, when the narrative has come full circle and the moment is recounted for the second time, the narrator's recollection is slightly modified: 'Juste au tournant de l'escalier, elle a dit doucement: «C'est fini»' (110). Ernaux has informed us that this modulation from 'd'une voix neutre' to 'doucement' was not incorporated in a conscious and deliberate manner into the text. She nevertheless acknowledges that the shift may well have a significance, albeit unconscious, and that it could bear interpretation. We would advance the hypothesis that the transition betokens a shift in personal response which came into being as the writing of the text progressed. The phrase 'd'une voix neutre' calls forth an emptiness or absence of feeling and reaction, a numbness. The adverb 'doucement', on the other hand, carries the suggestion of gentle acceptance.

The shift is from negative to positive, from detachment to involvement, and from separation to union. Within this tiny transition, perhaps, lies a reflection of the entire trajectory of *La Place*.

NOTES

(1)   This at least is the intention. We shall have cause at a later stage to consider whether intention is wholly matched by effect.

(2)   It is interesting that whereas towns of peripheral importance are named in full (Rouen, Le Havre, Dieppe, etc.), the towns that are the principal settings of the narrative are designated Y... and L... (*Une femme* makes clear that these stand for Yvetot and Lillebonne). As in the use of initials to designate the father, the narrator seems concerned to draw our attention away from the particular, and to give these locations a more generalised, representative significance.

(3)   Such fears were not imaginary: the progressive spread of stores and supermarkets, and the increased mobility of a car-owning population, steadily reduced the traditional dependence on the local shop.

(4)   These are the terms that Ernaux herself uses, both in her writings and in interviews, preferring on the whole to avoid the usual terminology (proletariat, bourgeoisie) of social classification.

(5)   An attitude of acceptance which ironically recalls the edifying formula impressed on the father by his childhood reading of *Le tour de la France par deux enfants:* 'Apprendre à toujours être heureux de notre sort' (30).

(6)   In *Une femme* the narrator says that at this age she thought her mother superior to her father 'parce qu'elle me paraissait plus proche que lui des maîtresses et des professeurs' (p. 58).

(7)   The 'ti' is a popular interrogative suffix. It appears to be derived from the inverted third-person form 'est-il?' or the colloquial 'C'est-il?' Perhaps the girls were trying out on Monsieur D... what they had read in Maupassant, whose stories involving the peasant folk of Normandy involve many such examples, plus variations such as 'J'sais-ti, mé?' for 'Est-ce que je sais?' and 'J'sieus-ti bu!' for 'Ai-je bu!'— see, *inter alia, L'Ivrogne, Le Père Milon, Le Père Amable, Tribunaux rustiques, Conte de Noël* and *Aux Champs.*

(8)   The two terms are explicitly linked by the narrator (95), with the implication that the second is attained as a direct consequence of the first.

(9)   The formulation of the sentence, exploiting the ambivalence of the *style indirect libre*, does not allow us to pinpoint the moment when this idea is born. Is it a question consciously formulated at the time by the teenage schoolgirl, or one framed retrospectively by the mature narrator? The latter is probably more likely. But either way, the important point is that a sense of guilt is obliquely acknowledged.

(10)   It is worth noting that the Capes, unlike any comparable British qualification, confers on its holder the lifetime guarantee of a job in the teaching profession. In that respect the diploma is more than a confirmation of ability: it enshrines permanence and security.

(11)   It seems likely, and Fernandez-Récatala (pp. 164-5) concurs, that the reference is to a work by Philippe Sollers (published in 1968, one year after the father's death), which deals with theories of writing and reading. If this is so, the full title of the text (*L'Ecriture et l'expérience des limites*) perhaps posits another level of unfounded anticipatory interest: was this also to be a work which explored the position of the writer seeking to give expression to social and cultural differences? Equally interesting is the fact that, in his critical edition of *La Place*, Michael Wetherill (p. 42) mentions 'L'Expérience des limites' as being one of several projected titles which Ernaux entertained before settling on that of *La Place*.

(12)   Interview with Jean-Jacques Gibert, 'Le Silence ou la Trahison?', *Révolution*, 260, 22 février 1988.

Une femme

Une femme was begun in April 1986, thirteen days after the
death of Ernaux's mother, and was completed ten months
later. Its composition spans a period of mourning, of
adjustment to the traumatising event which spurred the
narrator to begin writing (**21; 22; 23**). This is one obvious but
crucial way in which *Une femme* may be differentiated from
La Place (which was written, in its final form, fifteen years
after the death of Ernaux's father) and it accounts in part for
the more emotionally charged tone of *Une femme* compared
with *La Place*. The controlled urgency of *Une femme* also
derives from the nature of the relationship which the text
explores : the narrator's identification with her mother (as the
female parent and as the dominant partner in the parental
couple), the conflicts between mother and daughter in the
period of the narrator's adolescence and the confluence of
their lives in the years following the death of the narrator's
father, these lend an intensity to the mother-daughter
relationship which was not present in the relationship between
father and daughter.

For the narrator, to write about her mother in the weeks
and months following her mother's death is a natural and
indeed necessary part of the process of adjustment (**22**); the
decision to write and the emotions and ideas stimulated by the
ongoing process of writing, as well as the narrator's
reflections when she eventually concludes the work, are all
recorded in the text. The reader is thus led to reflect on the
value of writing as a means to confront bereavement and the
vortex of emotion which so often accompanies it. However, as
in *La Place*, the narrator maintains a dual perspective, seeking
to make a place both for the potent affective images of her
mother which are indelibly stamped in her psyche, and for a
more objective account of her mother's life. Early in the text
(**22-3**), the narrator identifies the two directions in which she
hopes to develop her exploration of her mother's existence.
One of these draws on her private images of her mother, and
produces a series of notations which selectively trace the
evolution of the relationship between mother and daughter;
the other attempts to parenthesize the mother-daughter
relationship in order to work towards a more objective
understanding of the mother's concrete experience in society.

In writing, the narrator hopes not only to achieve a better understanding of her mother and her own relationship with her, but also to grasp the meaning of her mother's existence within the network of social relations in twentieth-century France. It is Ernaux's conviction that the analysis of private experience and interpersonal relationships inevitably opens up the social domain; this is fundamental to her practice as a writer, as she herself likes to stress: 'Je pense—et c'est une de mes raisons d'écrire—que dans le destin individuel est contenu le social'.[1] This emphasis on the imbrication of personal existence and social reality rests on the understanding that individuals are rooted in their time and milieu, culturally, socially and historically situated in ways that may sometimes be hard to define, but which nevertheless condition their experience, attitudes, beliefs and perceptions. The historical situation and social position of the narrator's mother established the cultural parameters of her experience of motherhood and gave specific form to the customary drama between mother and daughter with its core dynamic of identification and separation. Factors relating to generation and class were fundamentally implicated in the tensions and difficulties between mother and daughter. These difficulties not only constitute a potential source of self-dissatisfaction and guilt for the narrator (and therefore a 'natural' focus for her attention), they also represent the most obvious points of insertion of the particular mother-daughter dyad into a wider social and historical context. If the narrator's most profound impulse, in writing, is to give pride of place to the luminous images of her mother which she carries in her mind (22-3; 52), she is nevertheless deeply committed to the attempt to understand the general or social implications of her mother's story. This very deliberate orientation towards the social domain is both an intellectual choice which allows the writer to seek greater understanding of her mother's existence and the contemporary social context (through patient reflection on the connections between the personal and the social) and a response to an emotional need to communicate, to find common ground with others, in order to break the numbing solitude of private grief (52).

We hope it is becoming apparent that there can be no clear-cut separation between the two dimensions— personal and social—which the author wishes to explore. This can be illustrated by reference to the long section of *Une femme* (24-

42, nineteen pages out of ninety-five) which is devoted to the story of the narrator's mother before the birth of her second—and only surviving—daughter in 1940. The narrator's concern to establish her mother's background and family history is obviously related to the interest in social context to which we have already drawn attention: only if the reader has a clear picture of the mother's origins and early years will s /he be in a position to envisage the broad sweep of her trajectory through life, and to perceive the social mechanisms which shaped her destiny. However, the account of the first thirty-four years of the mother's life is also necessary to the personal dimension of the narrator's project, the desire to explore and construct an account of her own relationship with her mother. There are two reasons for this. Firstly, the qualities and characteristics of Madame D...[2] as a mother are rooted in her personal history: both the specific nature of the emotional investment which she makes in her daughter and the cultural identity which excludes her from the middle-class world to which her daughter 'migrates' relate directly to her own formative experiences as a child and young adult. Secondly, in aiming to create an 'objective' picture of her mother (a picture in which the mother's life before the narrator's birth has an obvious and crucial place), the narrator recognizes her mother's autonomous existence outside the mother-daughter relationship, and thereby perhaps works towards her own emotional separation from the mother for whom she feels a profound attachment.

We have now identified three interwoven strands in the narrator's project which together constitute the thematic framework within which the narrative develops. These are the narrator's exploration of her relationship with her mother, her attempt psychically to integrate the fact of her mother's death (although this is not directly articulated, it is perhaps the fundamental trope of the narrative) and her concern to understand her mother's life and experience and point towards the social meaning which is implicit in her mother's story. In examining *Une femme*, we shall seek to identify the ways in which this triple perspective informs the text. The narrator's account of her mother's life is necessarily selective and specifically focalised through her own consciousness (we are reminded of these points by the frequent references to the ongoing process of writing), but within these inevitable limitations, she attempts to trace her mother's story and the evolution of the mother-daughter relationship through each of the intermediate stages of their development. The narrator's plans for the work which lies ahead (23) and her thoughts on its completion (103-106) frame the account of her mother's life; these passages, like the reflections on the process of writing and on the evolution of the narrator's feelings as the work progresses, connect past and present, writing and the attempt to decipher experience, and remind us that *Une femme* is fundamentally concerned with the potential and function of writing, its value (both for writer and readers) in the pursuit of understanding. Our analysis will follow the chronological structure which is adopted in the text and will trace the three narrative threads—the mother's story, the account of the evolving mother-daughter relationship and the unfolding drama of the narrator's feelings and understanding as she writes— which form the substance of *Une femme*. We shall be particularly concerned to explore the relationship between the personal and the social dimensions of the narrator's enquiry and to consider how far Ernaux succeeds in her attempt meaningfully to connect private experience and social meaning.

The mother's early life (pp. 24-43)

The narrator presents her mother as a unique individual with an unusually strong personality: she had a will of iron, immense vitality and a commitment to self-improvement which she maintained until she was well into her sixties. She was not a hapless victim , incapable of self-help in the face of difficult circumstances, nor did she lead a life of unredeemed wretchedness, but her freedom and her potential for social progress were ultimately constrained by economic factors and perhaps even more by the cultural disadvantage which was a legacy from her upbringing in a poor, semi-rural family in Normandy in the early years of the twentieth century (she was born in 1906). Her freedom was manifest to the extent that she rose above the condition to which she seemed destined ('la pauvreté sûrement, l'alcool peut-être'—34) and which indeed enveloped all her five brothers and sisters (*ibid.*); her subjection was evident above all in the shortfall in cultural capital which prevented her integration into the bourgeois world to which her daughter acceded by virtue of the education which her parents, as a matter of priority, provided for her.

In evoking her mother's existence as a young woman, the narrator stresses her mother's determination to 'make something of herself', and her relative success in this. More than any of her brothers and sisters, the narrator's mother bitterly resented the contradiction between her own positive asessment of her capacities and the negative social judgement which wrote her off as a member of an inferior class (**32**). As a young woman strongly motivated by a sense of injustice, the narrator's mother doggedly pursued her hopes of self-improvement. Faced with very limited job prospects, she chose factory work, a form of employment perceived to be more in tune with the times than the primitive drudgery of farm labouring, and less of an affront to personal dignity than the 'slavery' of going into service (**31**). If she adopted a personal style which announced her pleasure in novelty and change (short skirts, bobbed hair, a habit of looking others squarely in the eyes), she nevertheless respected conventional standards of conduct for young women (no smoking in the street, no intimate relationships with the opposite sex, a steady commitment to religion): only a serious and respectable girl could expect to make a favourable marriage, and marriage—a good one—was an essential step for a working girl anxious to improve her social standing.

The circumscribed nature of the young woman's freedom is already very apparent: factory work was a choice from a limited range of options, and it was a choice which she shared with virtually all the young people in the area (**31**), just as the narrator's grandfathers were both carters, and her grandmothers both home weavers (**24**; **36**); she constructed a persona which allowed for a limited expression of individuality, but which was ultimately constrained by the restrictive behavioural codes governing female behaviour in her society. It is true that these limitations are a particular manifestation of a universal phenomenon: freedom is always situated, we choose from the range of possibilities open to us, and we inevitably define ourselves by reference to the codes of behaviour which have currency in our society. However, it is obvious that these limitations fall very unequally on different generations and on different social classes: young people, and especially young women of the mother's class and time had some room for manoeuvre in the face of deprivation, but the enormous effort required to achieve anything beyond a very modest improvement in status must have discouraged all but the most determined.

With a carefully-chosen husband by her side (a gentle, hard-working man seven years her senior), Mme D... quickly realized that if marriage was a necessary condition for the social progress to which she aspired, it was by no means sufficient in itself to initiate real change (39); only with imagination and the acceptance of risk could the couple hope for a better life. It was Mme D..., more dynamic, ambitious and determined than her husband, who had the idea of starting up a modest business ('la seule aventure à sa mesure'—*ibid.*). In Lillebonne, as a young *patronne* of twenty-five, she was by no means unaware of the delicacy of her situation (making a living from clients who barely scraped a living themselves—40), but she enjoyed the social role of shopkeeper and indeed the power it carried (exchanging views with clients, arranging credit facilities, providing the basic necessities in wartime) and revelled in her financial and administrative responsibilities (she kept the accounts and undertook all the official negotiations associated with running a business). Her social standing and self-confidence were steadily enhanced: she learnt to speak with care, paid more attention to her appearance, began to read more widely (some modern classics such as Bernanos, Mauriac and Colette, as well as popular fiction) and eventually felt confident that she no longer betrayed her unsophisticated origins (41).

The fact that by this time Mme D... was a mother should not be overlooked. A first daughter, born in 1931, was to fall victim to diphtheria at the age of seven. In the wake of her death, the couple felt the need for a second child: 'ils ne voulaient qu'un seul enfant pour qu'il soit plus heureux'(42). This is a discreet but clear indication of the way in which the parents' (and especially the mother's) social ambitions would be invested in the child. Both M and Mme D... had known hardship in relatively large families, both were aware of their own precarious financial situation; the decision to have only one child was a very deliberate choice to protect the quality of family life which they could provide. It goes without saying that this is an eminently responsible attitude to parenthood, but its implications for the relationship between parents and child are not entirely unproblematical: to the extent that a child carries the weight of its parents' unfulfilled ambitions, the relationship between child and parents may become charged with conscious and unconscious feelings (of identification, anxiety, resentment, guilt, jealousy) which create conflicts and difficulties for all concerned. These are important considerations which should be borne in mind as we pursue our analysis of Mme D...'s social evolution: as a mother she would project herself into her daughter, vicariously experiencing through the younger woman's success a level of freedom which she herself could not hope to attain, and it is through her changing relationship with her upwardly mobile daughter that her cultural subjection becomes apparent.

Before we move on to consider the development of the mother-daughter relationship, it is worth noting the narrator's reflections as she records the fact of her own birth:

> La vie à nouveau, au début de 1940, elle attendait un autre enfant. Je naîtrai en septembre.
>
> Il me semble maintenant que j'écris sur ma mère pour, à mon tour, la mettre au monde. (43)

These lines present the dynamics of the mother-daughter relationship as an ongoing process of exchange. Conceiving another child restored the mother's vitality after the traumatic loss of her first daughter, while the narrator's project, to give her mother a literary existence, consciously reciprocates the mother's gift of life to her daughter. Mother and daughter form an intimate partnership in which each grounds and succours the other's existence; their lives interpenetrate and interconnect symbiotically.[3] However, as if to underline the strictly metaphorical nature of the existence which the narrator is able to confer upon her mother, the description of the mother-daughter relationship as an ongoing symbiosis is immediately followed by a series of notations which recall the fact of the mother's death and explore the narrator's current feelings about her bereavement. At first the narrator's words seem to suggest that she has achieved a measure of acceptance, a degree of objectivity in her attitude towards her mother's death: 'Il y a deux mois que j'ai commencé , en écrivant sur une feuille «ma mère est morte le lundi sept avril». C'est une phrase que je peux supporter désormais, et même lire sans éprouver une émotion différente de celle que j'aurais si cette phrase était de quelqu'un d'autre'(43). However, it is surely significant that the narrator's relative emotional equanimity is likened to the feelings she might experience if her words ('ma mère est morte') *had been written by someone else.* Perhaps, in 'writing her mother into literature', the narrator defers final acceptance of her mother's death and staves off the full impact of the potentially overwhelming sense of loss which it occasions. This interpretation is supported by the narrator's subsequent remarks about her feelings at this stage in the writing process. Firstly, the incompleteness of the process of adjustment and acceptance is strongly suggested by the recognition that memories or reminders of the last days of her mother's life are still too painful for the narrator to bear (**43**). Secondly, the work of writing involves the narrator in an aesthetic quest which, in a highly paradoxical double movement, both diffuses and concentrates the emotional energies which are generated by the narrator's loss, and which drive the work forward. On the one hand, the narrator's painstaking attention to formal aspects of the work (ordering of material, choice and combination of words) and her attempt to discover an elusive 'ideal order' as she writes (**43-4**) are totally absorbing and therefore presumably a distraction from grief; on the other hand, in constructing an account of her mother's life (and death), the narrator is inexorably writing her way towards the confrontation of loss. It is as if writing creates the space for a controlled encounter with the trauma of an unthinkable bereavement.

The daughter's childhood (pp. 44-59)

With the narrator's entry into the story, the focus shifts to the relationship between mother and daughter. The account of the years corresponding to the narrator's early childhood (up to 1945 when the narrator was five) draws both on Mme D...'s oral reconstructions of that period ('Ensuite, elle racontait les années de guerre comme un roman'—**45**) and on the narrator's own recollections, which foreground the magnetic attraction the mother held for her daughter. Seen through the eyes of her daughter, Mme D... was a striking red-haired woman full of vigour and vitality; she spoke loudly and often stridently, laughed expansively and sang readily. The narrator can still picture two of the dresses which her mother used to wear in those years, as well as her careful make-up and the tightly

laced corset, with its bow and rosette, into which Mme D...
habitually squeezed her ample figure. The child's fascination
with her mother's body knew no bounds, her sense of
identification was absolute: 'Rien de son corps ne m'a échappé.
Je croyais qu'en grandissant je serais elle'(46). The briefly
related anecdote which concludes this account of the narrator's
earliest years encapsulates the intense emotions which bind
young children to their parents, and especially (in a culture
where women are the primary care-takers) to their mothers.
Recalling a Sunday outing with her mother and father in
wartime, the narrator emphasizes the profound sense of
security which their presence created for her, as well as the
terror of separation and loss which she felt (particularly in
relation to her mother) when they were caught in shell fire as
they cycled home: 'je suis sur la barre du vélo de mon père et
elle descend la côte devant nous, droite sur la selle enfoncée
dans ses fesses. J'ai peur des obus et qu'elle meure. Il me semble
que nous étions tous les deux amoureux de ma mère'(*ibid.*).
Here, the mature narrator recognizes the desire—shorn of
none of its erotic connotations—which ran like an electric
current through the child's feelings for her mother.[4]

Like her ill-fated sister before her, the narrator failed to
prosper in the damp atmosphere of the valley, and in 1945 her
parents decided to leave Lillebonne and return to Yvetot,
hoping that in the windier climate of the plateau, their
daughter's health would improve. As might be expected, these
years of later childhood (between the ages of six and twelve)
are more expansively treated by the narrator than her pre-
school years. The mother retained her position at the centre of
her daughter's world, but increasingly we are shown a
relationship in which the daughter had to integrate negative
images of her mother: she learnt to weather the storm of her
mother's volatility and lack of discretion and to adapt to her
irritability and aggression. The narrator continued to identify
with her mother, but there is a suggestion that this
identification gave rise to feelings of intense discomfort and
embarrassment when Mme D... acted in a manner likely to
attract critical judgement from others (as when she drank too
much at a family party—50—or when she complained to a
teacher, in class time, about the expensive scarf which her
daughter had lost at school—48-9). As a child in postwar
Yvetot, the narrator was well supplied with toys and books,
there were regular visits to the dentist, the optician and the

chest specialist, she attended a private school and was fitted
out with good quality clothing and the best school equipment.
Mme D... was determined that her daughter should enjoy the
advantages she herself had been denied (51). However, this
constant drain on the family's limited resources caused Mme
D... (still the family accountant) much anxiety. She invested
willingly in her daughter's future, but she was unable to
comprehend the girl's carelessness with material possessions
(49), or her failure to appreciate the life which her parents had
made for her (52).

Physical intimacy between mother and daughter still had a
place in their relationship (notably on Sunday afternoons,
when the narrator was allowed to snuggle against her mother
as she rested in bed—49-50), but the mother's embraces,
although spontaneous and heartfelt, were often a sequel to the
harsh words, smacks and punches which frequently rained
down on the narrator (51). The threat of exclusion from her
mother's presence or attention seems to haunt the pages which
evoke this part of the narrator's childhood. She recalls a trip to
the seaside when her mother spent the day in the company of a
younger sister-in-law (perhaps a replacement for herself in the
child's eyes), totally absorbed in their joint activities and
conversation (49). She records the unhappiness and resentment
she felt in church, as her mother sang out her devotion to the
Virgin Mary, and affirmed her desire to be with her in heaven
(*ibid.*). The experience of exclusion from her mother's world
was in fact part of the narrator's daily experience. As the
daughter of a tradeswoman, she had to accept that she did not
have sole claim on her mother's time and attention:

> Elle était une mère commerçante, c'est-à-dire qu'elle
> appartenait d'abord aux clients qui nous 'faisaient vivre'. Il
> était défendu de la déranger quand elle servait (attentes
> derrière la porte séparant la boutique de la cuisine, pour avoir
> du fil à broder, la permission d'aller jouer, etc.). Si elle
> entendait trop de bruit, elle surgissait, donnait des claques
> sans un mot et repartait servir. [...] C'était une mère que tout
> le monde connaissait, publique en somme. (52-4)

It is significant that this passage is immediately preceded by a
paragraph which reaffirms the narrator's commitment to the
portrayal of the macrocosmic social dimension of her mother's
story:

> J'essaie de ne pas considérer la violence, les débordements de
> tendresse, les reproches de ma mère comme seulement des
> traits personnels de caractère, mais de les situer aussi dans
> son histoire et sa condition sociale. (52)

No doubt, as the narrator goes on to suggest, attentiveness to
the social and historical context of her mother's story opens
the way to an awareness of the connections between her
mother's life and the lives of others of her class and
generation, pointing towards social meaning. However, it
should not be forgotten that this reminder of the way the lives
of individuals are shaped by circumstance occurs in the middle
of a section of the narrative which for the first time confronts
potential sources of friction between mother and daughter. A
mother who does nothing to hide the swings in mood and
temper to which she is subject, who frequently administers
forceful smacks and slaps, and who routinely makes her child
wait for attention inevitably invites criticism in an age which is
highly conscious of child psychology, and often oppressively
prescriptive about standards of maternal care.[5] By drawing
attention to the material conditions of her mother's life (her
responsibility as a breadwinner, the punishing schedule she
imposed on herself, the tensions and uncertainties of her life as
a shopkeeper), the narrator reminds the reader, and perhaps
herself, that her mother's personality and behaviour can only
be properly understood in the context of the demanding and
stressful life which she led. More importantly however, it is
evident that Mme D...'s unpredictability and failure to be
constantly available to her daughter were far outweighed by
the positive qualities which she embodied. Her energy and
resourcefulness, her commitment to her work and the
satisfaction it afforded her, and above all her determination to
expand her own horizons and to encourage her daughter to do
likewise, these demonstrated that women, even as mothers,
carry these possibilities within themselves.

Mme D...'s efforts to provide the material support
necessary for her daughter's education and development were
matched by her determination to offer the cultural and
intellectual stimulation which the child also needed.
Commitment to her daughter's cultural development was a
natural continuation of her own pursuit of social and cultural
self-betterment, which gained pace as her financial situation
improved. Mme D... made a concerted effort to improve her

speech by eliminating grammatical errors and popular or regional expressions, she endeavoured to hide the unease she felt in middle-class company, she liked to look smart, and never left the house without carefully applying her make-up (56). She was desperate to extend her knowledge in every way open to her, and listened attentively whenever a conversation turned on a subject that was unfamiliar to her. For her, self-improvement was synonymous with learning; knowledge and books held a very special importance:

> S'élever, pour elle, c'était d'abord apprendre [...] et rien n'était plus beau que le savoir. Les livres étaient les seuls objets qu'elle manipulait avec précaution. Elle se lavait les mains avant de les toucher. (57)

In assessing the narrator's motivations for writing *Une femme*, and her feelings about the finished work (as these are recorded or suggested in the text) it will be important to take into account both her mother's high estimation of literature and her relative exclusion from it (indicated here by the veneration with which she treats books); we shall return to these points at a later stage in our analysis.

Mme D...'s thirst for knowledge created a powerful bond between mother and daughter. The narrator's studies were a daily subject of conversation; Mme D... would read the books recommended for her daughter, accompany her on visits to museums and cathedrals. The narrator's father did not share his wife's cultural aspirations; he saw no reason to change the habits and interests of a lifetime, and preferred to avoid situations and places where he felt 'out of place' (55). Her mother's vitality and determination, her openness to new experience, drew the narrator into an alliance from which her father was inevitably—if not wilfully—excluded:

> Tout en elle, son autorité, ses désirs et son ambition, allait dans le sens de l'école. Il y avait entre nous une connivence autour de la lecture, des poésies que je lui récitais, des gâteaux au salon de thé de Rouen, dont il était exclu. [...] Des deux, elle était la figure dominante, la loi. (58-9)

The use of the negatively charged term 'connivence' suggests a strong retrospective awareness of the prejudice caused to the narrator's relationship with her father as a result of the imbalance in her feelings towards her mother and her father (this sense of having failed her father or in some way let him down may be identified as crucial to the decision to write *L a Place*). However, the narrator is here concerned to stress the depth and range of her mother's influence on her daughter's developing subjectivity. In the standard Oedipal scenario, the maternal function in the development of the child's unconscious is limited to the realm of infancy, femininity is associated with passivity and lack, and it falls to the father to mediate the child's separation from the mother and entry into culture; by contrast, here the narrator affirms her continuing identification with her strong and dominant mother throughout the years of pre-adolescence: the all-powerful mother of infancy also presides over the child's discovery of the world beyond the family.[6]

The daughter's adolescence (pp. 59-65)

Following the usual pattern, closeness between mother and daughter gave way to misunderstanding and conflict in the narrator's adolescent years. Unsurprisingly, the daughter's developing sexuality was a major source of tension. As an adolescent, the narrator felt that her mother was disgusted by the changes in her daughter's body, that she could not bear to see her grow up and that she perceived only the risks of the relationships with boys which her daughter sought to establish. Inevitably, the narrator's desire for independence and experimentation strengthened in the face of the restrictions and interdictions imposed by her mother, and although her adolescent reaction to her mother's censorious attitude is only briefly evoked, the reader is left in no doubt about the force of hostility running from the adolescent to the older woman. Two remarks in particular take us to the heart of the narrator's negative feelings about her mother. The first of these exposes the violent rage aroused in the teenager by the mother who relentlessly blocked the daughter's progress precisely where she most needed space to develop as a woman; it is a barely veiled transposition of the infantile wish to destroy the 'bad' mother who frustrates the child's desire:[7] 'Quelquefois, je m'imaginais que sa mort ne m'aurait rien fait' (62). The typographical prominence given to this sentence (it is set apart from the paragraphs which precede and follow it) emphasizes its importance as a clue to the knot of conflicting emotions (past and present) which has to be untangled if the narrator is to come to terms with the death of her mother.

In the paragraph which follows this recognition of past hostility towards her mother, the narrator acknowledges that the adolescent battle over sexuality which she fought against her mother still has the power to unleash profound and violent emotions. She is well aware that to surrender to the pull of the extremes of emotional response (so that the mother is seen as all good or all bad) is to regress to a primitive level of perception; while images of the 'good' and the 'bad' mother vie for dominance, there can be no hope of accepting the mother as a person with strengths and weaknesses like anyone else. Despite this intellectual understanding of the need to transcend the extremes of subjective response, the narrator is unable to maintain any degree of objectivity as she recalls her mother's euphemistic words of warning about sex. The paragraph is concluded (and this is the second pointer to to the powerful sense of grievance which still haunts the narrator) by an image which focuses insistently on the African mothers whose obedience to a cultural norm of femininity leads them to collude in a process which mutilates their daughters' emerging identity as women:

> ... j'ai la même sensation de découragement qu'à seize ans, et, fugitivement, je confonds la femme qui a le plus marqué ma vie avec ces mères africaines serrant les bras de leur petite fille derrière son dos, pendant que la matrone exciseuse coupe le clitoris (62).[8]

It is significant that this identifies an emotion which is experienced *by the adult narrator as she writes.* The narrator's reconstruction of her adolescent relationship with her mother starkly juxtaposes references to her mother's recent experience of menopause with the evocation of her own sexual maturation, suggesting that retrospectively, the narrator is aware that her mother's need to adapt to her own changing sexuality may well have provoked anxieties and tensions (fear of ageing, perhaps unconscious jealousy of youthful sexuality) which made it difficult for her to accept her daughter's emerging sexuality (59-60). However, despite the understanding the narrator can now bring to bear on her mother's oppressive attitude to her daughter's teenage sexuality, it is a subject which continues to arouse negative emotions of great intensity: at this stage in the writing process, and on this crucial aspect of her relationship with her mother, the narrator is unable fully to overcome the resentment and anger which still tie her symbiotically to her mother: she is unable to establish the perspective which would allow her to let her mother go.

In considering the tensions which centred on the issue of sexuality, we have glimpsed something of the subterranean currents of feeling which connected mother and daughter and touched on an intensely personal dimension of their relationship. However, it is important to remember that even in this most private aspect of their relationship, social factors played a role that was far from insignificant. If Mme D... sought to curb her daughter's natural interest in sexuality, it was partly (perhaps mainly) in response to an obsessive fear that premature emotional entanglements would displace her daughter's interest in intellectual achievement or, in the most extreme scenario, that an unwanted pregnancy would put an end to a promising school career; Mme D...'s social ambitions for her daughter required the girl's academic success as a passport to a solid career and (secondarily) a good marriage (**69-70**). The generation gap also played its part in the respective attitudes towards sexuality held by mother and daughter. Mme D...'s reticence and wariness concerning sexuality may be seen as a legacy from the strict sexual conventions she had been taught to respect as a young woman, whereas her daughter's bid for sexual freedom in the mid-1950s (she was fifteen in 1955) has to be seen in the context of the newly emerging youth culture (originating in the U.S.A. and rapidly disseminated throughout Western Europe) which celebrated youthful rebelliousness and offered teenagers more aggressive models of sexuality (the narrator records her adolescent admiration of James Dean—**64**).

The importance of social and cultural factors in the relationship between mother and daughter can be seen even more clearly in the narrator's adolescent rejection of her mother as an intellectual companion and as a model of femininity. As the narrator's studies progressed, it became more and more difficult for her mother to participate in her daughter's discoveries and enthusiasms:

> Je découvrais qu'entre le désir de se cultiver et le fait de l'être,
> il y avait un gouffre. Ma mère avait besoin du dictionnaire
> pour dire qui était Van Gogh, des grands écrivains, elle ne
> connaissait que le nom. Elle ignorait le fonctionnement de
> mes études. (63)

In retrospect, the narrator understands that it was only
vicariously, through her daughter's intellectual and cultural
progress, that her mother could have access to the higher or
even intermediate reaches of culture. As an adolescent, she had
resented her mother's inability to continue to provide
intellectual stimulation, as if her mother had chosen her
exclusion from the cultural domain. Disillusionment was also
much in evidence in the narrator's adolescent perceptions of
her mother as a woman. Seduced by the image of femininity
which pervaded women's magazines[9] and which she
recognized in the mothers of her *petit-bourgeois* schoolfriends,
the narrator began to find her mother loud and crude,
unfeminine. A negative image displaced the profound
admiration which had been paramount amongst her childhood
feelings for her mother; identification still occurred, but now it
was resented as a source of humiliation:

> J'avais honte de sa manière brusque de parler et de se
> comporter, d'autant plus vivement que je sentais combien je
> lui ressemblais. Je lui faisais grief d'être ce que, en train
> d'émigrer dans un milieu différent, je cherchais à ne plus
> paraître. (63)

Mme D... could not understand why her daughter failed to
appreciate the privileged nature of the life her parents had
made for her; the narrator, as a teenager, could not understand
why her mother seemed to think that the only condition for
happiness was not to be sent to work in a factory at the age of
twelve (65). The narrator's retrospective account of her
adolescent years emphasizes the way in which her own
attitudes diverged dramatically from the priorities her mother
had adopted as a young woman. With hindsight, it is clear to
the narrator that in her adolescence she was already migrating
towards a different social class from that of her parents, and
that this could only lead to difficulties within the family;
mother and daughter were divided as much by class difference
as by the inevitable difference of generation: 'À certains
moments, elle avait dans sa fille en face d'elle une ennemie de

classe' (*ibid.*). Freed from basic material deprivation and the need to overcome it, the daughter's adolescent revolt was played out in an entirely different register from the one in which her mother's youthful energies had sought expression. The daughter despised social convention, religious observance, money (**64**): precisely those attitudes and areas of experience which her mother had accepted as crucial in the struggle for social advancement. As teenagers, both mother and daughter sought to rise above the social class into which they were born. However, whereas for Mme D... the only means to escape from the milieu in which she grew up was to build up financial capital ('gagner de l'argent et devenir aussi bien que les autres'—**65**), for her daughter it was above all through the acquisition of *cultural* capital (knowledge, aesthetic sensibility, the adoption of certain forms of speech, comportment and dress) that integration into a higher social class would be achieved.

It is true that this commitment to cultural self-improvement was a lesson the narrator had learnt from her mother ('s'élever, pour elle, c'était d'abord apprendre'—**57**), but Mme D... was unable to achieve a fundamental cultural reorientation for herself, given the limitations of her own formal education (she had, after all, been a factory worker at the age of twelve and a half—**29**) and the pervasive influence of the milieu in which she lived throughout her working life. Her daughter occupied a different, and in some ways more difficult (if more privileged) class position: she was located at the point of articulation between what in French are called the *classes dominantes* and the *classes dominées*, between those who enjoy status and privilege and hold political, social and cultural power, and those whose existence is played out at the lower end of the class spectrum, and who are socially disempowered by virtue of the economic and cultural deprivation (of varying degrees of severity) to which they are subject. In order to make the 'quantum leap' from a dominated to a dominant class identity, the daughter had to break with the cultural norms of her parents' class. A generation earlier, her parents had struggled to rise above the economic constraints under which their families laboured, in order to achieve a measure of independence and security, and the possibility of offering their child the advantages they had been denied. This point takes us to the heart of the tragic irony of the family's experience: the daughter's migration to a higher social class is in conformity with her parents' profound wishes for her development, yet it projects her into a social space which is inaccessible to them.

The years apart (pp. 65-75)

When the narrator left home to study in Rouen (first at the *lycée*, later at the university), the process drawing her away from her parents' way of life naturally accelerated. She would eventually marry a student from Bordeaux, start a family, move to Annecy with her husband and young son, take up a teaching post and bear a second child. These were years when the narrator's relationship with her mother appeared to be at its least intense: she was pleased to see her mother when she went home (relatively frequently as a student in Rouen, only once a year from Annecy), but did not miss her when she was away. Despite the emotional cost of acceding to her daughter's desire to leave home, Mme D... remained steadfast in her support of her daughter's academic ambitions; the narrator acknowledges her good fortune in having such a mother, one who was 'Prête à tous les sacrifices pour que j'aie une vie meilleure que la sienne, même le plus grand, que je me sépare d'elle'(65).

In terms of physical proximity and life-style, this separation was clearly very real, but the narrator's account of her relationship with her mother in these years when they led 'separate' lives suggests, at least if we read between the lines, that at a profound level the connection between mother and daughter retained its power. In the early months of her life away from home, the narrator acted out desires (presumably sexual ones) which her mother had forbidden, and jettisoned the sensible eating habits which she had learnt at home. The narrator suggests that the intensity of this reaction against her mother at this stage in her life allowed her to feel that she had worked through her hostility to achieve autonomy:

> Loin de son regard, je suis descendue au fond de ce qu'elle m'avait interdit, puis je me suis gavée de nourriture, puis j'ai cessé de manger pendant des semaines, jusqu'à l'éblouissement, avant de savoir être libre. J'ai oublié nos conflits. (65-6)

Significantly, it is unclear whether the older narrator shares the view of her younger self that is here articulated: retrospectively, does she feel that she did achieve real independence from her mother? Certainly the account of the earlier period emphasizes the reactive nature of this rebelliousness, which challenged her mother's authority in two of its most fundamental aspects (the taboo on sexuality and the regulation of eating habits), implying perhaps that the extreme defiance which is an obvious feature of this pattern of behaviour is one way of relating to her mother, not an expression of the daughter's independence. Paradoxically, the persistence of a deep-rooted connection between mother and daughter is further suggested by the fact that as a young woman the narrator 'forgot' the difficulties between her mother and herself. Psychoanalysis tells us that it is by 'forgetting' that we deal with experiences and feelings that we are unable to handle (this is the psychological mechanism known as repression).[10] If this idea is accepted, it may be that the 'forgotten' difficulties in the narrator's relationship with her mother in fact remained a very real (if hidden) source of resentment; only by facing up to her negative feelings towards her mother, and working through them, could the narrator hope to integrate the 'good' (remembered) and the 'bad' (repressed) images of her mother, and thus to see her realistically, in a way which would allow both mother and daughter the space to lead an autonomous existence. Perhaps this task was beyond the young woman who had only recently made the first tentative steps towards independence. For the older narrator, however, writing *Une femme* may be precisely the means to achieve this difficult integration of conflicting feelings towards the mother she has recently lost.

As a student, the narrator was drawn predominantly to the image of the good mother, self-sacrificing and totally committed to her daughter's well-being and success: 'J'étais certaine de son amour et de cette injustice: elle servait des pommes de terre et du lait du matin au soir pour que je sois assise dans un amphi à écouter parler de Platon' (66). This may be related to a subsequent comment: 'Jusqu'à vingt ans, j'ai pensé que c'était moi qui la faisais vieillir' (68) and to a passage from *La Place:* 'J'avais pour la première fois vécu loin de la maison, pendant deux mois, dans un monde jeune et libre. Mon père était vieux, crispé. Je ne me sentais plus le droit d'entrer à l'Université' (P, 86). The narrator's feeling that her youth and vitality somehow developed at the expense of her parents' health and vigour is a profound sign of her sense of responsibility (if not guilt) in the face of their existence and situation. The awareness of a fundamental inequality between parents and daughter, together with the debt of gratitude and no doubt the self-reproach which it carries with it, almost certainly lie at the root of Ernaux's desire to write, and go some way towards explaining her commitment to a kind of writing which foregrounds social injustice. This is a point to which we shall return.

The continuing existence of a powerful emotional bond between mother and daughter is further suggested by a series of notations relating to the years of 'separation': as a student, the narrator tended to go back home when she had emotional problems (even if she chose not to discuss them with her parents—66); her mother's pleasure in her daughter's return would be betrayed by the blush which came to her cheeks as her daughter entered the shop (*ibid.*), and by her attentiveness to her daughter's needs and interests (66-7); Mme D... developed the habit of referring to her husband as 'mon père' (67), as if to affirm the continuing viability of the triadic family unit (wife, husband, child), and took to wearing sombre colours (68), perhaps unconsciously mourning the 'loss' of her daughter (this suggestion may seem far-fetched, but its feasibility can be supported be reference to Mme D...'s renewed preference for light colours when she goes to live with her daughter's family in Annecy—80). Looking back, the narrator can see that while she remained unmarried, she still 'belonged' to her mother, even if her mother's claim on her was recognized as provisional by both parties (69). However, if the narrator's marriage signalled the end of an era in the mother-daughter relationship, it opened the door to a new kind of complicity, centred in the practicalities of setting up a household, and later in the well-being and progress of the narrator's children (70).

After her daughter's marriage, Mme D... showered the young couple with carefully chosen gifts, as if hoping to win through her generosity the love she needed but feared she might not be granted on her own merits; her letters frequently expressed the desire to offer her daughter more practical help, as she could if they lived in closer proximity (72), and, after the death of her husband in 1967, she could no longer hide her longing to become part of her daughter's family in Annecy (**74**). Thoughts of her mother's solitary existence, cut off from her grandchildren and excluded from the comfortable bourgeois existence she had worked to achieve for her daughter, weighed heavily on the narrator's conscience, to the point where she could not refuse her mother's desire to once again share her daughter's daily life; this sense of guilt in the face of the mother's (imagined) unhappiness is one of the most obvious signs that the narrator remained profoundly tied to her mother.

In the middle of this account of the years when mother and daughter led 'separate' lives (but when, if our analysis is correct, they remained profoundly connected), the narrator inserts a paragraph which records her feelings about the work in progress. It is a revealing passage which focuses on the difficulty the bereaved narrator experiences in letting her mother go; the mother is dead, but the separation of mother and daughter remains to be accomplished:

> On ne sait pas que j'écris sur elle. Mais je n'écris pas sur elle, j'ai plutôt l'impression de vivre avec elle dans un temps, des lieux, où elle est vivante. Quelquefois, dans la maison, il m'arrive de tomber sur des objets qui lui ont appartenu, avant-hier son dé à coudre, qu'elle mettait à son doigt tordu par une machine, à la corderie. Aussitôt le sentiment de sa mort me submerge, je suis dans le vrai temps où elle ne sera plus jamais. Dans ces conditions, 'sortir' un livre n'a pas de signification, sinon celle de la mort définitive de ma mère. Envie d'injurier ceux qui me demandent en souriant, «c'est pour quand votre prochain livre?» (**68-9**)

Here we encounter the first explicit recognition of the tension or contradiction which is inherent in the narrator's project. Both the secret nature of the process in which she is engaged and the fact that writing generates the illusion of her mother's presence suggest that the text is inscribed in the register of desire, expressing the narrator's longing for symbiotic union with her mother. However, this tropistic slide towards an illusory reunification is challenged by the intermittent but devastating realization of bereavement as an accomplished fact, triggering the narrator's reluctant understanding that she is writing her way into recognition of her mother's death, affirming the loss she has suffered and proclaiming the inevitability of ultimate separation.

Reunion? (pp. 75-81)

After three years of running the business alone following the death of her husband, Mme D... went to live with her daughter and her family in Annecy. Inevitably, there were problems of adjustment. The narrator does not draw back from the acknowledgement of her own negative feelings when she first caught sight of her mother on her arrival in Annecy: 'D'un seul coup, je me suis dit avec accablement, «maintenant je vais toujours vivre devant elle»' (75-6). From the perspective of the narrator's present existence in the wake of her mother's death, this remembered reflection must have carried a painful double irony. Firstly, she now suffers from the loss of the presence which was then perceived, at least in part, as a burden; secondly, although her mother is no longer physically present, she has lost none of her emotional importance for the narrator, whose thoughts and feelings are permeated by a deep fascination with her mother's existence. Perhaps even more after her mother's death than when she was alive, the narrator's image of her mother structures and organizes her consciousness. The bereaved narrator still needs to situate, define and justify herself in relation to her mother.

On Mme D...'s part, certain problems of adjustment were close to the surface, easily understood even if they were not susceptible to immediate resolution: she missed her busy life as a shopkeeper and the social persona it created for her; she regretted the loss of her capacity to earn her own living and suffered from the lack of a circle of friends and acquaintances (76). More profound and more intractable problems were rooted in the differences between the way of life to which Mme D... was accustomed, and her daughter's domestic routine and cultural environment. Mme D... had to learn to respect certain 'house rules' (tea towels were not to be dried on the radiators in the hall, her own handkerchief was not to be used for the children—*ibid.*), and she was hurt when her daughter and son-in-law disregarded, or even gently mocked, the preoccupations and concerns to which she attached importance (what the neighbours might think, news coverage of crimes and accidents). Certain aspects of her behaviour suggested that she felt an outsider, and indeed a subordinate, in her daughter's home: she would knock before entering a room where her son-in-law was watching television, and constantly asked for work, half-jokingly saying that she had to earn her keep. Only with time and thought was the narrator able to understand that her mother's sense of exclusion and unease originated in the cultural humiliation to which she was subjected in her daughter's household. Although she was a welcome addition to the family group, she had to adapt to a life-style which was alien to her, and to accept cultural norms which called into question the value of her own more popular tastes (innocently reading *Le Monde*, or listening to music by Bach, the young couple implicitly passed judgement on the popular press and mass market musical styles which Mme D... enjoyed). 'Jokingly' casting herself in the role of a paid servant was Mme D...'s strategy for dealing with this pervasive cultural oppression: the intangible but very real cultural domination to which she was subjected was transformed into an imaginary but more familiar and understandable form of oppression, the economic oppression experienced by the worker in relation to her employer (77-8); thus transposed, her instinctive refusal of humiliation (the narrator calls it 'une façon de se révolter'—78) could be openly expressed, communicated to her daughter in a disguised but potent form. This kind of response to a perceived (but not directly articulated) sense of inferiority can also be seen in Mme D...'s advice to her daughter on the eve of her wedding: «Tâche de bien tenir ton ménage, il ne faudrait pas qu'il te *renvoie*» (71). The mother's profound sense of identification with her daughter leads her to transpose onto her daughter her own sense of inferiority in relation to the cultural milieu of her son-in-law's family.

However, even in her mid-sixties, Mme D...'s resilience and vitality were such that she was able to overcome these initial difficulties and adapt to life in Annecy: she took pride in helping run the house, seeking to release her daughter as far as possible from routine domestic chores; she devoted herself to the care of her two young grandsons, spending hours every afternoon exploring the town with them. Gradually, she began to push back the cultural barriers which obstructed the process of integration in which she was engaged: she learnt to read 'quality' newspapers and magazines, to speak without vulgarity and to handle objects with discretion; she mastered bourgeois housekeeping practices, adjusted her appearance (losing weight and dressing more elegantly). This was a continuation of the process of cultural evolution she had carried through as a younger woman, as her financial and social situation improved. Her success in transforming her personal style suggests both her continued dynamism and openness to change, even as an older woman, and the extent to which a person's image and tastes (what might be called their cultural identity) are socially constructed, a product of the environment in which their existence is inscribed. When the family moved to a new town near Paris in the mid-1970s, Mme D... was unable to settle (initially they lived on a large new estate which had no community facilities), and she decided to return to her native Yvetot, moving into sheltered accommodation. In Yvetot, she was pleased to pick up the threads of her old life and to renew old acquaintances, but she was unused to a life of relative inactivity, and her studio flat, like the new estate which she had detested, seemed almost to have been designed to limit the horizons of its occupants (**80-81**). Only in the course of her extended visits to her daughter's family, and on the month-long holidays which she spent with them every year, was Mme D... able to rediscover her vitality and zest for life.

The last years (pp. 81-103)

When Mme D... was seventy-three, a serious accident left her unconscious for a week, and hospitalized for a much longer period. This setback paradoxically restored her willpower and fighting spirit (as if the threat to her existence had reawakened her appetite for life), although it forced her daughter to acknowledge, for the first time and with a deep sense of shock, her mother's vulnerability and mortality:

> Je regardais ses épaules nues, son corps que je voyais pour la première fois abandonné, dans la douleur. Il m'a semblé être devant la jeune femme qui avait accouché difficilement de moi, pendant une nuit de la guerre. Avec stupeur, je réalisais qu'elle pouvait mourir. (**85**)

This moment of insight took on the value of a premonition, pointing towards the final stages of the story of mother and daughter, when the primitive bond between the two women would be rediscovered and reaffirmed as an incapacitating disease propelled the mother relentlessy towards an ever more denuded level of existence.

Mme D... had held her own against the 'external' threat posed by the accident (86), but she stood no chance against the internal enemy—Alzheimer's disease—which was to ravage the last years of her life, forcing her step by step to surrender the place which she had made for herself with so much effort and determination. Eighteen pages of the text (86-103) chronicle the progress of this devastating and distressingly common form of dementia.[11] In the face of her mother's rapid decline and ever-increasing helplessness, the narrator was initially resentful and resisting: 'Je ne voulais pas qu'elle redevienne une petite fille, elle n'en avait pas le «droit»' (93). Learning to adjust to her mother's condition and to cope with her own distress was a slow and difficult process for the narrator: on one occasion the sight of her mother's exposed and vulnerable flesh provoked a painful memory of the security and well-being she had felt as a child in her mother's presence (96), and each visit to the hospital fuelled the anxiety she experienced as she watched her mother slide inexorably into an existence which seemed progressively less human (99). As the disease pursued its course, Mme D... lost even the most elementary cultural acquisitions, such as the desire to maintain at least a semblance of propriety in her eating habits or dress. Only basic instincts remained intact: to eat, to touch and be touched, to communicate, these desires persisted with great force, testifying to her stubborn attachment to life (98-101). The mother's hunger for care and attention was answered by the daughter's need to provide the physical comforts and emotional support which eased her mother's existence (101); at times she longed to do more, to devote herself entirely to the care of her mother (102). The powerful sense of identification with her mother which the narrator experienced at this time regenerated the visceral bond which had existed between mother and daughter in the narrator's childhood. The roles within the mother-daughter relationship were reversed (the daughter becoming maternally attentive to the needs of her failing, vulnerable mother, who had returned to the dependency of infancy), but the symbiosis between them remained strong, and indeed may have been stronger than it had been since the narrator's early years. Despite the galloping degeneration, both physical and mental, to which

Mme D... was subject, her death could only come too soon for
the daughter, who had once more grown dependent on her
mother's presence, unable to take in the enormity of the loss
which she knew to be inescapable. On a physical level, Mme
D...'s death effected the inevitable separation between mother
and daughter. Psychologically however, separation could not
be accomplished until the daughter was ready to let her mother
go. To what extent this was achieved through the writing of
Une femme is a question we must now address.

Between symbiosis and separation:
from the personal to the political

In the concluding four pages of the text, the narrative
'catches up with itself', evoking the narrator's feelings as she
contemplates her nearly completed manuscript. In a series of
seemingly disjointed and uncompromisingly minimal
notations, the narrator records some of her current perceptions
regarding her mother's existence, its ending and the literary
project which she felt impelled to undertake in the wake of her
mother's death. These perceptions are stated without being
developed or explained, and one line of thought is not explicitly
connected to others which precede or follow it. Each short
paragraph is set apart from the surrounding text, adding to the
impression of fragmentation and incompleteness, and seeming
to underline the narrator's incapacity to formulate a unified,
coherent, definitive assessment of the meaning of her mother's
life and death.

The questions which confront the narrator as she moves into
the final stage of the project which has occupied her for ten
months may be extrapolated from a careful reading of the text:
what delicate interplay between remembering and forgetting
has allowed her to come to terms with bereavement and what
sort of memories endure? how does the writing of *Une femme*
connect with Mme D...'s life of hardship and struggle? can
those who mourn find a way between symbiosis and
separation, between the desire to hold on to the past and the
need to let it go? In order to begin to understand the narrator's
response to these questions, the reader needs to be attentive to
the detail of the text, sensitive to the order in which ideas are

presented, and prepared to make connections between the impressions and feelings evoked as the narrator concludes her text and those to which reference is made at earlier stages in the narrative. The analysis which follows is intended to help the reader in this task.

Between the account of the events leading up to her mother's death and her concluding reflections, the narrator inserts a short paragraph which recalls her inability, in the days following her mother's death, to connect the experience of seeing her alive when she visited her for the last time and the experience of seeing her dead the next day. This is followed by a typographically isolated four-word sentence: 'Maintenant, tout est lié' (**103**). These strategically placed remarks echo the narrator's earlier comments about the necessity for her to confront and recount her mother's experience of Alzheimer's disease, despite (or rather because of) the emotional block which afflicts her as she approaches this part of her mother's story: 'je ne peux pas vivre sans unir par l'écriture la femme démente qu'elle est devenue, à celle forte et lumineuse qu'elle avait été' (**89**).

In this context, writing becomes a means to overcome the sense of discontinuity and disjunction which for the narrator accompanies the momentous personal changes signalled by her mother's progressive dementia and by her death. Paradoxically, she needs consciously to remember, to confront and articulate the painful experiences in order to 'forget', to let the past go and move on.[12] Thus, in recounting her memories of the last day of her mother's life, the narrator overcomes the psychological block which she first noted at a much earlier stage in the writing process (**43**); similarly, she is now able to observe her mother's old room (as seen from the car park of the rest home), whereas previously a return visit to the home was too painful to contemplate (*ibid.*). Ten months after her mother's death, the building no longer has the power to trigger gloom and anxiety in the narrator: 'l'immeuble m'a paru plus clair, presque accueillant' (**103**); she is astonished when she notices that another resident now occupies her mother's old room: this astonishment in the face of a development which is entirely predictable and logical suggests the extent to which her mother's death and the circumstances surrounding it remained fixed in the narrator's mind, as if sealed off from the processes of adaptation and renewal, until such a time as the narrator was ready to integrate the loss and move forward. Moreover, it is clear that the shift which has occurred in the narrator's consciousness involves a fundamental reassessment of her own position as an individual on a journey, as we all are, from birth to death. Our parents, who precede us on this journey through time, not only provide a link back to our origins in the past, they also project us forward in time, insofar as their destiny, and ultimately their death, prefigure our own. These connections are perhaps most acutely felt by daughters in respect of their mothers, since in the case of girls the emotional bonding which normally occurs between an infant and its mother is reinforced by subsequent gender identification and by the high affective charge which usually remains a feature of mother-daughter relationships. Certainly, in the narrator's case, there is an easy slippage from the notion that someone has taken her mother's place in the rest home to the idea that soon it will be her turn to confront old age and death: 'J'ai pensé aussi qu'un jour, dans les années 2000, je serais l'une de ces femmes qui attendent le dîner en pliant et dépliant leur serviette, ici ou autre part'(103-104).

The following paragraph records a more radical identification of daughter with mother; here, the transformative power of dream takes over from the more restricted play of the waking imagination. It should be noted that this is one dream selected from the almost uninterrupted sequence of dreams about her mother which the narrator experiences in the months when she is writing *Une femme*. It is surely significant that the dream recorded in the text contains no simple, clearly defined image of the mother, although the narrator appears to feel sustained by her mother's presence, as if the mother's strength and love flow ubiquitously in the waters of the river which contain and support the daughter's body. The only specific reference to the mother occurs in the curious image which concludes the account of the dream: the daughter's sexual organs—which are those of a child—are also the sexual organs of her mother (104). If the narrator has chosen to record this image, it is perhaps because it juxtaposes the sexuality of mother and daughter, broaching a domain that was a major source of conflict and discord between them: the most powerfully hostile feelings towards her mother which the narrator acknowledges relate precisely to Mme D...'s attempted repression of her daughter's adolescent sexuality (61; 62). It is surely no accident that the dream brings mother and daughter together at the 'sticking point' in their relationship, the one area of the daughter's existence where she was denied her mother's acceptance and approval. Dream interpretation is a notoriously hazardous activity, and it seems presumptuous to confer meaning where the narrator has chosen not to. Inevitably, however, readers will ask themselves what the dream means, and this response may be said to be invited by the inclusion of the dream in the text. We propose therefore to compromise by sketching two directions which interpretation might take, leaving readers to choose between them or imagine others.

On the one hand, we might see the dream as pointing to the emergence of new strengths in the narrator: sustained by the memory of her mother's love (symbolized by the supporting waters of the river) and seeing beyond the old hostility between mother and daughter to the underlying bond (suggested by the shared genitalia) which gave their relationship depth and solidity, the daughter's 'new self' (represented by the pre-pubescent body, trailing strands of plants like an afterbirth) is ready to confront existence without the reassurance of her mother's physical presence. On the other hand, we might see the dream as expressing the regressive desires of a woman who is not yet ready to let her mother go: unconsciously longing for the bliss of infantile surrender to the magical, beneficent mother (symbolized by the river), prepared to give up her bid for sexual autonomy in order to win the mother's acceptance and approval (a renunciation of the right to self-determination symbolized by the immature sexual organs, those of a girl whose sexuality has not yet brought her into open conflict with her mother, and by the juxtaposition of the genitalia of mother and daughter) the daughter retreats from the necessity for growth and change in the wake of her mother's death. Whether or not one of these interpretations is accepted (and both are tentative), the narrator's choice to include this dream, and the reference to its place in a sequence of dreams about her mother, clearly point to the magnetic attraction the mother continues to hold for the daughter. Whatever position is consciously adopted by the narrator, it will not provide a firm and stable basis for development unless it takes account of her profound need to establish a vital connection between her own present existence and the life of her deceased mother.

Dream gives way to waking illusion as the narrator records her occasional and always fleeting impression that her mother is about to walk downstairs and settle down with her sewing. This recalls the narrator's earlier surrender to the illusion of her mother's presence (68-9) although, unlike its precursor, the later manifestation of this unconscious refusal of her mother's death in no way compromises the narrator's ongoing awareness of the true situation. No doubt it is this clear advance of adaptation to reality over illusion which prompts the narrator to remark that these fleeting impressions of her mother's continuing presence may be 'la première forme de l'oubli' (104). If the memory of her mother's presence remains, for the moment, very vivid in the narrator's mind, some of the incidental circumstances surrounding her death remain accessible only because they are recorded in the text, where they can be rediscovered at will (105). The familiar details that constitute the presence of a loved one may be more firmly rooted in our consciousness than casual observations which are peripheral to our emotional life, but even our most precious memories must inevitably fade.

Time is not of course the only threat to cherished memories: they may also be undermined by new insights which disturb our reading of the past. The anecdote about the sexual conduct of the narrator's mother before she was married (105) does indeed suggest a sexual adventurousness and a willingness to break with accepted codes of behaviour, which the narrator has not previously perceived in her mother (34; 38, and P, 36-7). The information which might lead the narrator to revise her assessment of her mother's attitude to sexuality has only recently come to her attention, and it is plainly unwelcome: 'Maintenant que ma mère est morte, je voudrais n'apprendre rien de plus sur elle que ce que j'ai su pendant qu'elle vivait' (105). Why then does she choose to record the anecdote, and moreover draw attention to it by stating her own negative feelings about it? We would suggest that the reasons for this apparently paradoxical decision are that the narrator wishes to emphasize the personal, selective and inevitably incomplete nature of the account of her mother's life which she has produced, while at the same time asserting her strong commitment to her own version (now a written account) of her mother's story. These claims require further consideration. The narrator's account of her mother's life is constructed from within the limitations of her own perceptions and understanding and therefore subject to errors, misinterpretations and omissions, of which this detail about her mother's sexual behaviour as a young woman is just one example. If we pursue these considerations to their logical conclusion, we shall be led to accept the view that the narrator's account has a fictional dimension. This would in fact be entirely consistent with the narrator's project as she initially defines it: 'Ce que j'espère écrire de plus juste se situe sans doute à la jointure du familial et du social, du *mythe* et de l'histoire'(**23**: italics supplied).

The narrator's strong sense of attachment to her own account, however incomplete, may also be usefully juxtaposed with her initial definition of her project, which is concluded by a reflection on the relationship between literature and truth:

> Mon projet est de nature littéraire, puisqu'il s'agit de chercher une vérité sur ma mère qui ne peut être atteinte que par des mots. (C'est-à-dire que ni les photos, ni mes souvenirs, ni les témoignages de la famille ne peuvent me donner cette vérité.) Mais je souhaite rester, d'une certaine façon, au-dessous de la littérature'. (**23**)

This passage identifies writing as the *only* means to arrive at the truth which the narrator seeks (the relativity of 'une vérité' should be noted); photographs, personal memories and relatives' accounts of the past cannot provide access to this truth: these resources all have their place in the process of investigation and analysis, but are seen as preliminary and preparatory to the quest for authenticity and meaning which is fundamental to the work of literary composition as the narrator conceives it. The references to the writing of the text which are a recurrent feature of *Une femme* serve to draw our attention to the process of literary creation, which is often slow and uncertain. The narrator emphasizes her preoccupation with the selection and organisation of material and with the choice and disposition of vocabulary (**43**). She refers to the elusive 'ordre idéal' which she seeks to create (**43-4**) and which, if it could be attained, would make the text uniquely meaningful for her, definitive as a personal account of lived experience despite its recognized relativity (as a narrative which has its basis in subjective understanding and aesthetic judgement, and as an inevitably approximate description of reality), replicating the process which has already occurred in the account of her father's death in *La Place* (**73**; **P**, 103-110).

However, it is important not to lose sight of the closing remark in the quotation cited above : 'Mais je souhaite rester, d'une certaine façon, au-dessous de la littérature'(23). The structural and formal considerations which the narrator identifies as essential to her practice as a writer should not be seen primarily as a sign of her commitment to the pursuit of an aesthetically accomplished style; rather, they are an indication of the author's determination to express, as precisely and faithfully as possible, the lived experience which she evokes. The cultural disadvantage to which Mme D... was subject manifested itself above all in her relative exclusion from dominant modes of discourse. Although painfully aware of her linguistic inadequacy, and desperately anxious to overcome it, she could never have hoped to match the linguistic sophistication which her daughter acquired through education. In these circumstances, an account of her life which employed the stylistic features usually associated with 'literary' modes of expression (imagery and symbolism, lyrical description, the use of the past historic to recount the past) would inevitably distort the mother's experience and accentuate the gap between language and reality. For Ernaux, writing is aligned with affection and respect for the world of her parents, and with the desire faithfully to transcribe that world which is now lost to her (doubly lost, through her changed class status and through their death).[13] The work of composition crucially involves a concerted effort to find the most authentic form of expression and the most telling arrangement of material; it is itself the means by which perceptions are organised and meaning constructed. The completed work becomes the vehicle for a personal poetic truth.

To return to the sequence of reflections which focuses loosely on the theme of memory, and which constitutes the first part of the conclusion of *Une femme*, one striking image remains to be explored. The image in question, which follows the narrator's recognition of the displeasure with which she receives 'new' information about her mother, evokes the predominant form of the narrator's memory of her mother ten months after her death: 'Son image tend à redevenir celle que je m'imagine avoir eue d'elle dans ma petite enfance, une ombre large et blanche au-dessus de moi'(**105**). The narrator herself underlines the imagined infantile source of this impression, and there seems every reason to accept the accuracy of this observation, which could be supported by reference to the substantial body of work (predominantly but by no means only psychoanalytical in orientation) on the enduring legacy of the early mother-child relationship.[14] The image in question takes on particular resonance when it is set alongside the definition of the project which becomes *Une femme*.

The narrator's intention, articulated early in the text, is twofold. Firstly, she seeks to give expression to the primal images of her mother which permeate her consciousness. These images are powerfully charged with affective meaning, but because they translate the daughter's profound emotional response to her mother, they have only a limited capacity to illuminate the concrete reality of her mother's existence; anarchic and free-floating (they privilege certain of her mother's characteristics while neglecting many others and they cannot be matched to a specific moment in time), they are literally the stuff of dreams (**22-3**). The image of the mother on the penultimate page of the text ('une ombre large et blanche...'), like the dream image which juxtaposes the sexual organs of mother and daughter, must clearly be aligned with that part of the narrator's initial project which seeks to give expression to the daughter's most private and most deeply rooted responses to her mother. As much when she concludes the narrative as when she began writing, these are the narrator's dominant maternal images. The second constituent element of the narrator's project involves close attention to her mother's historical situation and to the concrete manifestations of her existence. While this involves an attempt to create a picture of her mother's existence outside the mother-daughter relationship, it does not *exclude* that relationship, and in any case the perceptions and understanding which make the account possible are of course the narrator's own. As Adrienne Rich has said: 'It is hard to write about my own mother. Whatever I do write, it is my story I am telling, my version of the past' (*Of Woman Born*, p. 221). Much of *Une femme* is devoted to the patient reconstruction of the mother's attitudes, behaviour and appearance over the years. It would seem that the work of reconstruction draws largely on the narrator's recollections which, if not fully and easily accessible to the conscious mind, can nevertheless be recuperated through a process of concentrated introspection (**P**, 100); the inevitably fragmented and incomplete picture of the past which memory necessarily provides is clearly signalled by the frequent gaps in the text. In the case of the mother's existence before her daughter's birth, the narrator's memories of her mother's stories of her early life and information gleaned from relatives form the basis of the narrative.[15] In the account of the mother's life both before and after her daughter's birth, remembered or reported details are no doubt augmented by a degree of imaginative reconstruction (the fictional element to which reference has already been made).

If we compare the two aspects of the narrator's project, and the different kinds of memory on which they draw—the powerful but obscure images which are the vehicle of the primitive and enduring symbiotic connection between mother and daughter, and the more specific and focused images which relate to the mother's concrete presence in the world—it does not seem unreasonable to suggest that the text serves a different function for the two kinds of memory. The memories which relate to the mother's evolving personality and familial and social role are closer to the surface of consciousness, and therefore no doubt less enduring, than the profound images—existing perhaps only on the margins of consciousness—which are the mark of the primitive bond between mother and daughter, and which are so much a part of the daughter's being that she will carry them with her as long as she lives. This interpretation may be supported by reference to the 'ombre large et blanche'(**105**) which is the narrator's predominant maternal image, even after a ten-month period of concentrated analysis of her memories of her mother. For the narrator, anxious to 'lutter contre la disparition, contre l'oubli' (interview with Jean Royer), writing about her mother provides the opportunity to work on her memories, to give them distilled and concentrated form. Those memories which are closer to the surface of consciousness may be fixed and preserved in the words of the text, while the diffuse and mysterious images which issue from less accessible areas of the mind may be acknowledged and given at least token form and substance as part of the narrator's literary homage to her mother.

At this point, as we approach the final page of *Une femme* and the narrator's concluding reflections on the text she has created and its relationship to her bereavement, it is worth bearing in mind the quotation which Ernaux has chosen as the epigraph for *Une femme*, and which draws attention to the inevitable presence of contradiction at the heart of human experience: 'C'est une erreur de prétendre que la contradiction est inconcevable, car c'est bien dans la douleur du vivant qu'elle a son existence réelle'.[16] It may safely be said that contradiction informs the narrator's project at the deepest level and in a wide variety of ways. It is evident in the tension between life and death which is implicit in the narrator's instinctive recourse to writing as a strategy for dealing with the painful fact of her mother's death. Through the process of writing, the narrator not only perpetuates the memory of her mother, in a sense extending her existence, but also struggles towards the recovery of her own emotional equilibrium: writing creates a space where she can work through her own grief and thereby survive.[17] However, if in some respects the text may be aligned with survival, and therefore with life, it nevertheless returns insistently to the subject of death, since it recognizes and affirms the reality of the mother's death. As she writes, the narrator's grief is held in check by the sense of her mother's presence, but the work of composition comes to an end, breaking the connection between mother and daughter forged in the process of writing. The completion and publication of the work signify a definitive recognition of bereavement, an affirmation of the loss sustained by the narrator; the mother's death dissolves the narrator's last remaining link with the world of her childhood (**106**). Yet it may also be said that, as a published text circulating in the public domain, *Une femme* serves to mark and honour, to write into literature and thereby to preserve, the vital bond between mother and daughter.

When Mme. D... dies, part of the narrator dies with her. While this identification is only natural in a daughter whose subjectivity is closely bound up with her mother's existence, and who reads her own future in her mother's destiny, it is exacerbated in the narrator's case by her choice as a writer to project herself into the mother as a character whose story she seeks to tell. However, in thus projecting herself into her mother, the narrator reciprocates her mother's prior and massive emotional investment in her daughter. This means that presence and an enduring legacy can be set in the balance against absence and loss; if the mother may be said to live on in her daughter, life is not wholly vanquished by death. Here we encounter another manifestation of contradiction. In so far as the narrator seeks to take stock of her relationship with her mother and thereby to identify what she might carry forward from her, she must inevitably confront the ambivalence which, as in all close relationships, marked the bond between her mother and herself. Thus, although admiration and deep attachment figure prominently in the narrator's account of her relationship with her mother, she also acknowledges having felt resentment, hostility and contempt towards her; moreover, although these negatively-charged emotions reached a climax in the narrator's teenage years (a notoriously difficult phase in the relationship between a mother and her daughter), they were present in an attenuated form at other times (for example in the daughter's spontaneous misgivings when her mother moved to Annecy—76), and those which run deepest retain their power even as the narrator writes her mother's story (62).

The necessity for the bereaved to confront their ambivalent emotions towards the deceased is widely accepted by psychoanalysts and psychotherapists working in this field. The ability to integrate conflicting feelings towards a deceased person is most crucial when close relationships are severed by death, and may be particularly problematical in the case of daughters who lose their mothers, as the daughter's symbiotic ties to her mother (ties which may be positively or negatively charged, or both) may have remained strong while the mother was alive. An adult woman who denies ambivalence in her feelings towards her mother, who sees her mother (whether the mother is alive or dead) as all good or all bad, or who alternates between these two extremes, remains trapped in a pattern of primitive responses first established in relation to the mother of her infancy. Only if a bereaved daughter can see her deceased mother as a whole person, necessarily imperfect because she was human, will she be able to achieve the separation which is necessary if she is to move on; only if she is able to acknowledge and accept having felt a degree of hostility towards her mother, and to perceive this as reasonable, will she be free to make a forward-looking adjustment to bereavement, perhaps by identifying within herself the good inheritance she has received from her mother. The narrator of *Une femme*, while acknowledging the tensions and difficulties in her relationship with her mother, is able to adopt a perspective which allows for failings on both sides (although it seems likely, and this is a point to which we shall return, that her own sense of guilt is only partially assuaged in this process). Furthermore, the narrator identifies qualities in her

mother (courage, unflagging energy, determination, the will to
struggle for what she wanted in the face of unfavourable odds)
which any daughter would be proud to inherit, and which we
might identify in the narrator's own pursuit of creative
excellence. It is perhaps in and through her life as a writer that
the narrator is most clearly her mother's daughter: Mme D...
loved to read, venerated books and longed for her daughter to
become an intellectual; she took spontaneous pleasure in
sharing and giving, a quality which the narrator perceives in
her own commitment to writing (**106**). Like Simone de Beauvoir
(whose importance for the narrator may be inferred from the
coupling of Beauvoir's death with that of Mme D...),[18] but
more crucially, because her example was all-pervading and
present from the start, Mme D... fired her daughter's
enthusiasm for intellectual enquiry and achievement. Although
both these women are now dead, their ideals have been
internalized by the narrator, who thus carries forward their
memory and their influence.

In the opening sentence of the penultimate paragraph of the
text, the narrator offers an assessment of the kind of work she
has produced: 'Ceci n'est pas une biographie, ni un roman
naturellement, peut-être quelque chose entre la littérature, la
sociologie et l'histoire' (**106**). Presumably, these remarks also
serve to indicate how the narrator would like the text to be
read: our attention is diverted away from the realm of the
personal and the imaginary and towards the general and
documentary dimensions of the work. The lines which follow,
and which conclude *Une femme*, serve as a reminder of the
divisive nature of the class structure in which the existence of
mother and daughter is inscribed. Thus, and here again we
encounter contradiction, although the narrator's career as a
writer is a fulfilment of her mother's wishes for her, enabling
her to feel her mother's presence in what she is and does, it is
also a sign of the cultural disjunction which developed between
mother and daughter as a result of the narrator's education. In
writing her mother's story and situating her existence in the
context of the social history of her time, the narrator gives her
mother what she was denied in her lifetime, a place in the
world of words and ideas. This is presented as a subjectively
necessary and productive undertaking, allowing the narrator
to develop a sense of her mother's continuing supportive
presence and to reaffirm the specificity of her own divided
cultural identity: 'Il fallait que ma mère, née dans un milieu

dominé, dont elle a voulu sortir, devienne histoire, pour que je me sente moins seule et factice dans le monde dominant des mots et des idées où, selon son désir, je suis passée'(*ibid.*). It is obvious that the narrator has no wish to elide the cultural differences which came between her mother and herself, nor to mask the cultural oppression suffered by her mother. The writing and publication of *Une femme* allow the narrator both to affirm the connection and confront the contradiction between the successful writer she has become and the dominated milieu in which she grew up. In a talk that she gave to students and staff at Southampton University, Ernaux identified her own cross-class experience and the desire to address the question of social inequality as fundamental to her practice as a writer:

> Que peut écrire un écrivain qui a appartenu au monde dominé quand il arrive finalement dans le monde bourgeois et surtout dans une littérature qui est en France essentiellement bourgeoise à 80%? Donc tous mes livres tournent un petit peu autour de ça...

It is in this context that we can understand the element of *dénonciation* which Ernaux has repeatedly identified as an important feature of her writing. *La Place* and *Une femme* draw attention to one of the key mechanisms whereby social and cultural oppression is constructed and maintained. The domain of 'high culture' (of which literature is a major constituent) largely excludes working-class and lower-middle-class people, both through its relative inaccessibility to those who lack intellectual training and through its choice and treatment of material: the existence of those who are humiliated and oppressed by the dominant social order, if it figures at all in literature, is likely to be represented from a middle-class and therefore *external* perspective which distorts the experience which it seeks to portray and, perhaps more importantly, confirms its status as inferior:

> J'avais l'impression que la littérature portait sur ce monde et ces gens d'une classe dominée—d'autres disent populaire—un regard extérieur qui ne me paraissait pas juste. Mes livres répondent, certes, au désir personnel que j'avais de faire entrer mes parents dans la littérature. Mais avec eux, c'est aussi toute une classe sociale que j'emmène. (Interview with Jean Royer)

When Ernaux evokes her feelings in relation to her own
separation from the dominated social class to which she once
belonged, she has a tendency to use words such as
responsibility, guilt, betrayal; she has spoken of a desire to
make reparation, of a sense of *duty* or *mission,*[19] which lead
her to attempt to convey, as faithfully as possible, the
experience of people of her parents' class and to write in such a
way that her texts will not exclude those who lack literary and
intellectual sophistication. These points merit further
consideration. If we leave aside, for the moment, the subject of
Ernaux's motivations as a writer (the role of guilt and her
sense of mission), it is important to reflect upon the
relationship between language and reality. In representing
working-class and lower-middle-class existence, Ernaux does
not claim to eliminate the inevitable gap between language and
reality, but merely to represent reality in such a way as to
reduce distortion to a minimum: 'J'ai essayé le moins possible
de falsifier'.[20] This is a crucial distinction, not only because
language cannot give unmediated access to reality, but also
because the middle-class writer, whatever her class
background, cannot simply jettison the cultural identity
acquired through education and professional status in order to
step into the shoes of people from a less privileged milieu.
Furthermore, the disjunction between the existence of the
author and her parents is perhaps most evident in the realm of
language. Ernaux cannot unproblematically reproduce the
language of a class to which she no longer belongs, and in any
case to attempt to do so would be to de-emphasize the
contradiction (between her own social position and that of her
parents) which is fundamental both to *La Place* and *Une
femme.* She therefore adopts two strategies which enable her
to reach towards the language which she once shared with her
parents, without renouncing the linguistic control and
correctness which have become natural to her. Firstly, words
and expressions commonly used by her parents are
incorporated in a quite substantial way into the text (they are
identified by the use of italics of quotation marks); secondly, she
consciously adopts a style which is reminiscent of the letters
exchanged between herself and her mother or other members
of the family, a style which is 'neutral' and unadorned, flatly
'reporting' essential developments without explanation or
elaboration, and without the embellishments (imagery, irony,
lyricism) which are commonplace in literature (interview with

Jean-Jacques Gibert). Just as Ernaux's letters to her family
avoided the stylistic flourishes which would have been seen as
an assertion of superiority and a barrier to communication (**P**,
89-90), so *La Place* and *Une femme* strive for directness and
clarity of expression, in the hope that the texts will remain
open to readers across the class spectrum:

> Je pense vraiment que l'on peut dire les choses les plus
> subtiles, les plus menues [...] dans une langue et d'une
> manière que tout le monde... enfin un maximum de gens, les
> comprennent [...] ; que tout le monde ne comprendra pas de
> la même façon, mais que chacun pourra en tirer quelque
> chose. (Interview with Loraine Day)

At this point, we may usefully return to Ernaux's question: 'que
peut écrire un écrivain qui a appartenu au monde dominé...?'
and to the feelings of guilt and betrayal, and the compensatory
sense of mission which she has recognised as fundamental to
her identity as a writer. Ernaux's sense of *betrayal* originates in
her awareness of the extent to which she had forgotten or
repressed the cultural legacy which she inherited from her
family; she feels *responsible* towards those she has 'left
behind', and hopes to *make reparation* by acknowledging her
own social origins and by writing in a way that recognises and
indeed foregrounds (both through choice of subject matter and
style) the existence of those whose lives are played out at the
lower end of the social hierarchy: this becomes one of her key
motivations as a writer, taking on the value of a *duty* or
mission.

It is clear that from Ernaux's own point of view, writing is
an effective strategy for dealing with the powerful and
potentially destructive feelings engendered by her separation
from the class into which she was born. In *La Place* and *Une
femme*, the narrator opens up a dialogue with her parents;
belated and one-sided as this dialogue is, it nevertheless
affirms her solidarity with the family and the milieu in which
she grew to maturity. However, she emphasises that she does
not see writing as a kind of therapy, allowing her to purge
troublesome emotions and resolve painful inner contradictions.
Guilt is not so much a compulsive and unwelcome emotion as
one that is freely chosen and consciously assumed, the sign,
with writing, of a continuing fidelity to the uncomfortable
truths that she has perceived:

> L'écriture n'est pas une psychanalyse. Au bout de quatre livres, je ne suis pas débarrassée de ce qui est fondamental. Peut-être vais-je trouver d'autres biais pour évoquer cette coupure de façon différente. (Interview with Jean-Jacques Gibert)

Writing thus becomes a means to confront and hold in focus the reality of conflict, separation and loss. However, if writing issues from the perception of dissatisfaction and lack, and from the (unrealisable) desire to overcome this,[21] it is also essentially a means of communication. As published works, *La Place* and *Une femme* mark an intervention in the cultural domain; they allow the author to communicate with her many readers and to assert the reality of social difference. Of course, literature cannot overcome separation and loss in personal relationships, any more than it can close the gap between different social classes. However, as an intellectual production belonging in the cultural domain, Ernaux's writing can at least register symbolic dissent and point towards certain fundamental social inequalities which continue to divide the French nation (and how many others?) in the final decades of the twentieth century. Ernaux has acknowledged that she sees her writing as 'une forme de lutte, d'action' (interview with Jean Royer); it is for readers to judge, and indeed to determine, through their responses to Ernaux's work, to what extent this contestatory and ultimately political perspective may usefully be applied to *La Place* and *Une femme*.

NOTES

(1) Jean Royer, 'Pour que s'abolisse la barrière entre la littérature et la vie', *Le Devoir*, 26 mars 1988.

(2) The narrator does not refer to her mother in this way; we use it for convenience and because it is consistent with the narrator's use of initials to designate her parents and relatives from her mother's side, whose surname began with the same letter (see for example **F**, 32 and **P**, 21, 111).

(3) Symbiosis is a biological term signifying the interdependence of two organisms which cannot live without each other.
The concept of symbiosis in mother-child relationships was developed by Margaret Mahler in the 1970s. The initial physical and emotional closeness of mother and infant sets up a pattern

of psychological interdependence which is not always fully
outgrown later in life. Persisting mother-child symbiosis can be a
source of reassurance and security, but it can also submerge and
stifle individuality, hindering the necessary separation of
mother and child.

(4)   Late in his career, Freud recognized that his earlier theories had
underestimated the passion and tenacity of the girl's early
attachment to her mother.

(5)   Ernaux's novel *La Femme gelée* (pp. 156-8) identifies mother-
blaming psychoanalytical theories and prescriptive child-rearing
manuals as significant elements in the array of social pressures
which exert an oppressive and alienating influence on the
narrator.

(6)   The very interesting psychoanalytical implications of this family
constellation (enterprising, dominant mother and retiring,
unobtrusive father) in Ernaux's work have been explored by
Simone Flammang in an unpublished dissertation entitled
L'Aliénation dans l'œuvre d'Annie Ernaux (L'Athénée de
Luxembourg, 1988). Annie Ernaux kindly loaned us her copy of
this text.

(7)   The idea that infants relate to their mothers in a profoundly
ambivalent way is fundamental to Melanie Klein's theory of
child development: 'The mother in the pre-Oedipal or preverbal
period is a highly ambiguous figure. The child sees her as either
the magical nurturer or as the denying witch. Both seem
omnipotent in the child's perception. Therefore a split into the
good and the bad mother will occur, according to Melanie Klein'
(*Women Analyze Women*, p. 12).

(8)   Clitoridectomy (the excision of the clitoris) is still widely
practised in African countries (being routinely carried out by
women on girls who may be as young as seven), where it is seen
as a rite of passage into femininity.

(9)   *L'Écho de la mode* is mentioned specifically. This magazine,
which is no longer published, focused predominantly on
housekeeping skills, presenting an image of women as dutiful
wives and mothers. It had a strong Catholic and traditionalist
bias and appealed mainly to lower-middle-class readers. Ernaux's
three novels (*Les Armoires vides, Ce qu'ils disent ou rien* and
La Femme gelée) identify cultural representations of women as a
significant influence on the development of female subjectivity.

(10)   Eric Berne's definition of repression reads as follows: 'Pushing
something into the unconscious, or keeping something from
becoming conscious. Repression keeps the individual from
being in a continual state of confusion by preventing him from
becoming aware of many things, though what is forgotten or

unknown still remains an active force in the unconscious part of the mind' (*A Layman's Guide to Psychiatry and Psychoanalysis*, p. 406).

(11) 'Alzheimer's disease [...] is the most common form of dementia, and it's estimated that 500,000 people in the UK suffer from it. It's a cruel and progressive physical deterioration of the brain, which obliterates the personality of the sufferer as the ability to remember, to think, to learn and to reason vanish. The causes are unknown and as yet there is no cure' (Jonathan Miller, writing in the *Radio Times*, 18-24 November 1989, p. 105).

(12) Although there is clearly a similarity between the process which is here described and psychoanalytical practice, several important factors differentiate the two; these may be summarized as follows: (i) the narrator practises self-analysis, alone; (ii) her pursuit of self-knowledge is crucially related to an aesthetic quest: release is achieved by giving literary expression to lived experience which the conscious mind is otherwise unable to integrate; (iii) the painful past experience which she explores is not repressed in the psychoanalytical sense (i.e. it is not unconscious), rather it is available to consciousness which is however initially loath to confront it.

(13) 'Je suis née [...] dans un monde dominé culturellement, ce qui veut dire que j'ai une expérience du monde qui m'a façonnée comme elle façonne tout le monde, mais d'une certaine façon je veux la retranscrire... Je sens, j'ai toujours senti ça, vouloir la retranscrire, dans l'écriture. Non pas seulement dans le contenu mais aussi dans la forme' (Ernaux, speaking at Southampton University, 10 March 1988).

(14) Dorothy Dinnerstein for example has claimed that even as adults we may unconsciously feel our mothers to be 'engulfing' and 'nebulously overwhelming' (*The Rocking of the Cradle and the Ruling of the World*, p. 175), while Nancy Friday has written: 'In the unconscious where the first connection was forged, the mother of our infancy never dies' (*My Mother My Self*, p. 456).

(15) Specific reference to the mother's stories of her early life is made only occasionally (e.g. **F**, 36), but the importance of the recollection of her mother's words (both as a source of material and as a strategy in the quest for authenticity) is evident from the narrator's frequent citation of her mother's expressions. However, Ernaux pointed out in a talk at Winchester College (10 March 1988) that her mother was relatively reticent about her childhood, because she sought to rise above the social condition which she knew as a child. For this reason, in writing *Une femme*, Ernaux may have drawn more significantly on information gleaned from relatives (e.g. **F**, 25, 38) than was the case when she was working on *La Place*.

(16)   Ernaux found this quotation in Roger Garaudy's *La Pensée de Hegel* (Paris: Bordas, 1966, p. 147); it is taken from Hegel's *Science de la logique*, tr. S. Jankélévitch (Paris: Aubier, 1947), vol. 2, p. 481).

(17)   As Ernaux commented in conversation with Isabelle Larrivée, 'l'écriture est une lutte contre la mort. Il fallait à la fois faire vivre ma mère et me faire vivre moi pour surmonter le deuil' ('Droit de passage', *Voir*, 24-30 mars 1988).

(18)   Ernaux has spoken of her discovery of Beauvoir's work as a revelation. Specifically, it is to the reading of *Le Deuxième Sexe* as a student in the early 1960s that Ernaux attributes her awakening to the injustice of the feminine condition (a theme which is explored in her novels).

(19)   In a discussion at Winchester College, Ernaux commented as follows on this aspect of her motivation as a writer: 'Tout le monde préfère être plus libre, avoir le savoir, tout le monde préfère être plus riche, mais dans ce passage, on laisse finalement de côté tout son premier monde. [...] Ecrire, c'est un recours, c'est faire quelque chose dans le sens de la réparation... [...] Il n'y a pas de trahison volontaire, mais en s'éloignant de sa famille, même sans le vouloir, on peut éprouver de la culpabilité. [...] A travers mon père, j'avais l'impression de parler pour d'autres gens aussi, (pour) tous ceux qui continuent de vivre au-dessous de la littérature et dont on parle très peu. Donc c'était une sorte de devoir, je n'en ai jamais douté, pas plus que pour ma mère...'. See also Ernaux's interview with Jean-Jacques Gibert ('Le Silence ou la Trahison?', *Révolution*, 260, 22 février 1988).

(20)   Gibert, *loc. cit.*

(21)   'L'écriture, c'est quand même une forme d'un manque, d'un vide quelque part qui se remplit avec de l'écriture. Donc, comme le vide, on ne peut pas le combler réellement, avec la réalité' (talk at Winchester College); also: 'Il y a dans la vie des choses qui vous poussent presque inexorablement vers l'écriture, par le fait que non seulement la vie déçoit, même la vie vécue déçoit—l'espèce de vide, d'insatisfaction—mais en même temps, par une sorte de retour, même tout ce qui pourrait certainement être bien dans la vie est continuellement vécue comme une insatisfaction' (unpublished interview with Loraine Day, 26 November 1987).

Glossary

For reasons of space, this is a selective list which concentrates on cultural or historical references, lesser-known proper names, and colloquial or regional language. As a general rule, vocabulary and expressions which can be found in *Le Petit Robert*, or which are glossed in Ernaux's texts or our own, are not included.

Almanach Vermot (**P**, 33)   collection of humorous stories.

années noires de la crise (**F**, 42)   international economic crisis of the 1930s, which took hold in France in 1931.

apéro (**P**, 53)   (colloquial) aperitif.

'assommoir' (**P**, 54)   low drinking den (after Zola's novel [1877] of the same name).

Autant en emporte le vent (**F**, 45)   Margaret Mitchell's *Gone with the Wind*, published 1936.

avec ça? (**P**, 40)   'Will there be anything else?'

Avventura [L'] (**F**, 70)   1959 film directed by Michelangelo Antonioni (b. 1912), known for his 'highbrow' films with little narrative content.

Bagout [forts en] (**P**, 62)   local patter merchants.

balatum (**P**, 57)   kind of linoleum.

Bécassine (**P**, 60)   naive Breton folk heroine appearing in children's books.

bleu (**P**, 43)   working overalls.

Blum [Léon] (**F**, 42)   writer and prominent socialist (1872-1950); premier of the Popular Front government (1936-1937), which brought in a substantial package of social reforms (holidays with pay, the 40-hour week, the recognition of collective bargaining).

bordel (**F**, 87)   horrid place.

boudoirs (**P**, 54)   sugar-coated 'champagne biscuits'.

Bouglione (**P**, 65)   famous circus.

Bourvil (**P**, 60)   comic film actor.

Brassens [Georges] (**F**, 64)   writer and singer (1921-1981) of offbeat anticonformist songs; *La mauvaise réputation* is a song dating from the early 1950s.

Caddie (P, 113) supermarket trolley (brand name).
cadres moyens (P, 85) people in middle management.
Capes (P, 11) *Certificat d'aptitude pédagogique à l'enseignement secondaire:* teaching diploma.
Carmel (P, 77) Carmelite convent / monastery.
cauchoise (P, 62) originating from the Pays de Caux (northern Normandy).
centre Leclerc (F, 81) no-frills food supermarket.
C.E.T. (P, 114) *Collège d'enseignement technique.*
Charles [le grand] (P, 88) General de Gaulle, who returned to power as President in 1958, pledging to solve the Algerian crisis.
Clair [René] (P, 66) *nouvelle vague* film director (1898-1981).
CM2 (P, 69) *Cours Moyen deuxième année* (final year of primary school).
Confidences (F, 49) now-defunct women's magazine featuring photo-romance stories, with a mainly working-class readership.
Coop (P, 41) Co-op; chain of foodstores.
Croix-de-Feu (P, 42) extremist right-wing organisation.
cru [lait] (P, 99) fresh from the cow.
Cuirassé Potemkine (P, 32) *The Battleship Potemkin.* 1925 Russian film classic: a mutiny is sparked off by the quality of the food.
cul de poule [bouche en] (P, 18) affected haughty expression
CX (P, 70; F, 84) top model in the Citroën range from the late seventies until the arrival of the XM in 1989.

Delly (F, 41) pseudonym of Jeanne and Frédéric Petitjean de la Rosière, authors of many popular romantic novels, particularly between 1913 and 1928.
demain (P,76) play on words ('à deux mains'), hence the reply 'à deux pieds'.
dépassait / dépassées (P, 56; F, 28) downgraded / hand-me-down (family usage).
Desmarets, Marie-Anne (P, 79) writer of popular novelettes
'dirlo' (P, 80) slang for *directeur.*
DS (P, 70) top model in the Citroën range from the fifties to the seventies.

Écho de la Mode first appeared as *Le Petit Journal de la Mode* in 1880, later known as *L'Écho de la Mode;* covered the usual range of 'feminine' interests; folded in 1955.

École des fans (F, 103) — popular Sunday afternoon TV programme; Jacques Martin is host to an audience of parents and children; the latter perform songs, dances, party tricks, etc.

élève-maîtresse (P, 89) — trainee teacher.

envoyer dire (F, 32) — negated: not to mince your words.

épicerie Fauchon (F, 74) — upmarket grocery store; main branch in Place de la Madeleine, Paris.

exode (F, 44) — flight of French civilians from invading German troops, May-June 1940.

Faire (s'en) (P, 66) — to get worked up.

faire (se) (P, 59) — *ce qui se fait*—what is fashionable.

Familistère (P, 41) — chain of corner shops.

Fernandel (F, 58) — stage name of Fernand Contandin (1903-1971); popular comic film actor.

France-Dimanche (F, 86) — popular weekly newspaper, similar in style to *The People* or *News of the World.*

Front populaire (P, 22) — left-wing alliance (Communists, Socialists, Radicals) which won the elections in May 1936.

Galette des rois (P, 33) — traditional cake eaten on Twelfth Night.

gazinière (P, 41) — gas stove (brand name).

goutte-à-goutte (F, 85) — saline drip.

Gray, Daniel (P, 79) — writer of popular novelettes.

grivoiseries (P, 65) — spicy tales.

guerre d'Algérie (P, 88; F, 64) — the Algerian struggle for independence from France (1954-62).

Hérisson [Le] (F, 58) — popular weekly satirical newspaper, founded 1937; targets are political.

Himalaya (P, 65) — switchback.

H.L.M. (P, 85) — *Habitation à loyer modéré:* low-priced rented accommodation.

Infarctus (F, 73) — heart attack.

Laputa (P, 73) — airborne island in *Gulliver's Travels.*

Lilliputien (P, 65) — midget (see above).

lotissement (F, 80, 84) — housing development.

Maître de forges [Le] (**F**, 33)   play adapted by the popular writer Georges Ohnet (1848-1918), who dealt with romantic entanglements between aristocracy and middle class, from his novel of the same name (1882).

malabars (**P**, 99)   bubble gum.

malins de la ville (**P**, 35)   streetwise townies.

Mariano, Luis (**P**, 79)   sentimental singer.

mire (**F**, 86)   test card.

Mode du jour [La] (**F**, 49)   women's magazine, focusing on fashion and house-keeping skills; ceased publication in the 1950s.

monter la tête [se] (**F**, 64)   to get carried away, to get big ideas.

muguet du premier mai (**F**, 97)   sprigs of lily-of-the-valley, sold for charity on Labour Day.

Nez [en avoir un coup dans le] (**F**, 34-5),   to have had one too many.

Nouvelles Galeries (**F**, 56)   big department store.

Nouvel Observateur (**F**, 79)   topical weekly left-wing magazine.

O.A.S. (**P**, 88)   *Organisation de l'armée secrète:* terrorist body opposed to the independence of Algeria.

Opinel (**P**, 68)   general-purpose wood-handled penknife (brand name).

orientation (**P**, 114)   what one is training to be.

Payer [s'en] (**F**, 33)   (colloquial) to have a good time.

payer de toupet [se] (**F**, 56)   (colloquial and old-fashioned) to have the nerve.

pesée du pain (**F**, 27)   piece of bread added to make up the weight of a loaf.

péter plus haut qu'on l'a (**P**, 59)   to get ideas above one's station.

'pet de travers' (**P**, 106)   nothing serious.

Petit Écho de la Mode (**F**, 30)   very popular women's Sunday magazine;

Pierre l'Ermite (**F**, 41)   pseudonym of Edmond Loutil (1863-1959); priest whose edifying Catholic novels remained popular until the 1930s.

Poujade [Pierre] (**P**, 75)   founder in the 1950s of the *Union de Défense des Commerçants et Artisans de France*, a militant right-wing movement opposed to economic change, and supported by small shopkeepers.

Printemps (**F**, 56)	big department store.
pubs (**F**, 97)	adverts.
putsch des généraux (**P**, 88)	in 1961, four generals sought unsuccessfully to seize power in Algiers, in opposition to de Gaulle.

Quarts (faire les) (**P**, 43-4)	to do shift work
'quat'sous' (**F**, 28)	family euphemism for female genitalia, especially the clitoris.
quitte chez soi à se laisser aller (**P**, 63)	though anyone could let themselves go at home.

Rasière (**P**, 33)	(regional) old dry measure (= approx. 2 bushels).
Redoute [La] (**F**, 87)	mail-order catalogue appearing twice yearly.
revue ('on est gens de') (**P**, 85)	'We'll see you again.'
rincettes (cuver rincettes et surincettes) (**P**, 53)	to sleep off the effects of 'one for the road' and 'just one more for the road'.
Riquita jolie fleur de Java (**F**, 45)	jolly love-song, vintage 1926; popular at wedding receptions.
rodées (**P**, 76)	corny, well-worn (jokes).
Rodier [un chemisier] (**F**, 80)	a fairly expensive label: classic styling.
Roger la honte (**F**, 33)	popular play by Jules Mary (1851-1922); adapted by the author (1888) from his novel of the same name.

Saint Guillaume du Désert (**P**, 27)	Saint Guilelmus: late 8th / 9th-century saint, credited with miracles.
saint Riquier (**P**, 27)	Saint Richarius: 7th-century saint, credited with healing powers.
sale [au] (**P**, 19)	dirty clothes basket.
sarrau (**F**, 98)	pinafore.
secrétaire Louis-Philippe (**P**, 98)	nineteenth-century writing desk.
simili-marbre (**P**, 57)	imitation marble.
skaï (**F**, 94)	vinyl 'leathercloth'.

Tati [Jacques] (**P**, 66)	director and comic film actor
t.c. (**F**, 14)	*taxe comprise.*
Temps des cerises [Le] (**F**, 45)	ballad composed by the poet and social activist Jean-Baptiste Clément (1866).
Terre-Mère (**P**, 33)	Mother Earth: the perception of the Earth as the bounteous source of all life.
tort (**P**, 76)	play on words: 'le tort chez moi' / le torché, moi' = 'I've had my arse wiped'.

Tour de la France par deux   by 'G. Bruno', pseudonym of Madame
enfants [*Le*] (**P**, 30)   Alfred Fouillée, wife of the French
    philosopher, who wrote several works
    of *lecture courante,* school primers
    encouraging sentiments of moral and
    civic responsibility. This 'cours moyen'
    reader, subtitled 'Devoir et Patrie', was
    a phenomenal bestseller: published in
    the same year as Zola's *L'Assommoir,*
    it bids fair to have outsold this
    masterpiece of Naturalism, if the
    figure quoted on the 1977 facsimile
    reprint (Paris: Librairie Académique E.
    Belin)—'8.460e mille'—is anything to
    go by.

trois-huit des raffineries (**P**, 56)   shifts (day, night and 'back').

troisième âge (**F**, 82)   retirement.

Untel (**P**, 73)   so-and-so.

Vedette (**P**, 70)   Simca car.

vent [faire un] (**P**, 43)   to 'break wind' (i.e. fart).

vignettes (**P**, 99)   sticky labels affixed to prescribed
    medicament boxes, used to claim
    reimbursement from the Social
    Security.

Villequier (**F**, 57)   village on the Seine, near Rouen; site
    of the grave of Victor Hugo's daughter,
    Léopoldine, and her husband, who
    both drowned there in 1843. Their
    death was commemorated in *Les
    Contemplations:* 'À Villequier'.

Zéro (**P**, 71)   useless creature.

Zig-Zag (**P**, 88)   cigarette papers (brand name).

36 (**P**, 44)   (see 'Front populaire').

4 CV (**P**, 56)   small Renault car popular in postwar
    years.

Bibliography

Unless otherwise indicated, books written in French are published in Paris, and those written in English are published in London.

Works by Ernaux

Les Armoires vides. Gallimard, 1974.

Ce qu'ils disent ou rien. Gallimard, 1977.

La Femme gelée. Gallimard, 1981.

La Place. Gallimard, 1983.

Une femme. Gallimard, 1987.

Passion simple. Gallimard, 1991.

Journal du dehors. Gallimard, 1993.

Interviews with Ernaux and critical material relating to her work

Alphant, Marianne	'*Une femme* apparaît', *Libération*, 19 janvier 1988.
Day, Loraine	'Class, Sexuality and Subjectivity in Annie Ernaux's *Les Armoires vides*', in *Contemporary French Fiction by Women: Feminist Perspectives*, ed. Atack, M. and Powrie, P. (Manchester University Press, 1990), pp. 41-55.
Ernaux, Annie	Reply to a question concerning the literary context in which she places herself, in *The Review of Contemporary Fiction* (Elmwood Pk., Ill.: The Dalkey Archive Press), IX (Spring 1989), 'New French Fiction', pp. 210-11.
Fernandez-Récatala, Denis	*Annie Ernaux.* Monaco: Éd. du Rocher, 1994.
Ferney, Frédéric	'Annie Ernaux: la cérémonie des adieux' *Le Figaro*, 8 February 1988.
Gibert, Jean-Jacques	'Le Silence ou la trahison?', *Révolution*, 260, 22 février, 1988.

Larrivée, Isabelle   'Droit de passage',*Voir*, 24-30 mars 1988.

Royer, Jean   'Pour que s'abolisse la barrière entre la
                            littérature et la vie', *Le Devoir*, 26 mars 1988.

Wetherill, P.M. (ed.)   *La Place*. Methuen, 1987.

Other works

Apter, Terri   *Altered Loves: Mothers and Daughters during
                            Adolescence*. Hemel Hempstead: Harvester
                            Wheatsheaf, 1990.

Baruch, Elaine H.   *Women Analyze Women*. Hemel Hempstead,
& Serrano,   Harvester Wheatsheaf, 1988.
Lucienne J. (eds.)

Beauvoir, Simone de   *Une mort très douce*. Gallimard, 1964.

Berne, Eric   *A Layman's Guide to Psychiatry and
                            Psychoanalysis*. Harmondsworth: Penguin,
                            1986.

Davison, Ray (ed.)   *Une mort très douce*. Methuen, 1986.

Dinnerstein,   *The Rocking of the Cradle and the Ruling of the
Dorothy   World*. The Women's Press, 1987; first publ. in
                            the U.S.A. as *The Mermaid and the Minotaur:
                            Sexual Arrangements and Human Malaise* [1976].

Freud, Sigmund   'Female sexuality', in *On Sexuality*.
                            Harmondsworth: Penguin, 1987 (The Pelican
                            Freud Library, Vol. 7).

Friday, Nancy   *My Mother My Self: The Daughter's Search for
                            Identity*. Fontana, 1989 [1977].

Hinton, John   *Dying*. Harmondsworth: Penguin, 1967.

Lejeune, Philippe   *Je est un autre: l'autobiographie, de la littérature
                            aux médias* (Seuil, 1980), particularly
                            'L'autobiographie de ceux qui n'écrivent pas',
                            (pp. 229-316).

Mahler, M.S., Pine, F.,   *The Psychological Birth of the Human Infant*. New
& Bergman, A.   York: Basic Books, 1975.

Philippe, Anne   *Je l'écoute respirer*. Gallimard, 1984.

Rich, Adrienne   *Of Woman Born: Motherhood as Experience and
                            Institution*. Virago, 1984 [1976].